THE A-Z GUIDE TO BLACK OPPRESSION

[ELEXUS JIONDE]

AN <u>INTELEXUAL MEDIA</u> BOOK

To Tamir Rice, for changing my life.

To Anne Moody, for giving me endless courage.

TABLE OF CONTENTS

WHY DOES AMERICA NEED THIS BOOK?

When the dust finally settled on my mentions after my controversial 9/11 twitter thread last Fall, one sentiment lingered on my mind more than any compliment, insult, or death threat I received. It was rubbed across my twitter and Facebook like marinade, reeking of ignorance and vitriol. The accusation was so ridiculous and unimaginable that it was worse than the confederate flag wearing country boys who told me to hang myself and wished my first child would get cancer.

"Black people love pulling the race card."
"You don't see the (*insert Jews, Italians, Spanish, etc) playing the victim role!"
"GET OVER IT! You're not victims anymore."

While most saw my thread as educational or powerful, there was a diverse group of contrarians who believed my goal was to victimize the black race. They thought I brought up the past to give black people excuses for our failures and setbacks. To put it lamely, they assumed that I was stuffing the deck with race cards. Over the next few months whenever I tweeted a thread that pertained to historical cause and effect I continued to be accused of emboldening black victimhood. People would tell me to get off twitter and "go do something" if I really cared about black issues. Go do what? Yell at people on street corners? No, not even that. Rather than point out how historical events and attitudes have framed contemporary values and practices, they'd prefer me to allow toxic facets of black oppression to continue going unchecked and unexplained. They

would prefer that I use a privilege I've been granted- a large social media platform- to strictly talk about celebrity gossip, $200 dates, and my sexual preferences. They don't want me to use my privilege to help other black people because they don't think black people are facing unique problems. It isn't just white people thinking like this, either. Black people blind to the big elephant in the room wander into my mentions quite often. Both black and white accusations that I am "pulling the race card" by talking about the past are rooted in ignorance. They truly dont fathom the magnitude of black oppression, believing it to be a thing of America's past. They have zero grasp of the sick truth that this country is built on the subjugation of its darkest citizens.

The A-Z Guide to Black Oppression was born from the desire to expose how white supremacy has tainted America from the root. I want people to understand how the cards are stacked against black Americans. The point of this book is not to victimize black people. It is to wake us up so that we can STOP being victims of a system that has spanned centuries. From divisions to voter abuse, I want my people to be informed on the ways that we are being held back from true racial progression. I want ya'll to see how connected everything is. This book will give us all a solid foundation of information on how oppression keeps us from reaching our full potential. Systematic oppression is a grizzly and complex behemoth that includes more than a few curveballs. Everyone needs to understand it at a deeper level than dictionary comprehension. It is not something only useful for engineers or scientists or doctors or call center associates or plumbers... it is something everyone must grasp. Unfortunately American grade school curriculum is appallingly subpar, which means too many black people walk around ignorant of the problems we face as a unit. Some hardened intellectuals want to keep the crucial concepts in this book esoteric, roped off like the Hennessy filled VIP section of an exclusive club. But I'm sick of it. This will only continue to work against our favor. Often the black community wonders aloud what we can do about our status in this country. The answer is nothing until we're all on the same page about what the issues are. Without widespread enlightenment of what we are facing, we will never have widespread and meaningful discussions, action, or change. Because there are many pro-black people who subconsciously oppress other blacks, this book also seeks to inform you on the tentacles of black oppression that we have been socialized into perpetuating at the benefit of white supremacy.

Though some experiences within will be shared by other groups, this book is not about *people of color*, *minorities*, *poor whites*, or anyone else. It is about a people who were imported to America, subjugated, and targeted because of their status as black human beings. I'm perfectly aware that white supremacy has had a stranglehold on most of the world for centuries, and it did not start or begin with American slaves and their descendants. But this isn't the Oppression Olympics. I know that my people across the diaspora will be able to parallel concepts, events, and tactics in the following pages to their own unique ancestral experiences that I wouldn't dare presume to be an expert on. With that being said, this book is strictly about black oppression in America. I am a black woman in this country and I'm tired of hearing about race cards.

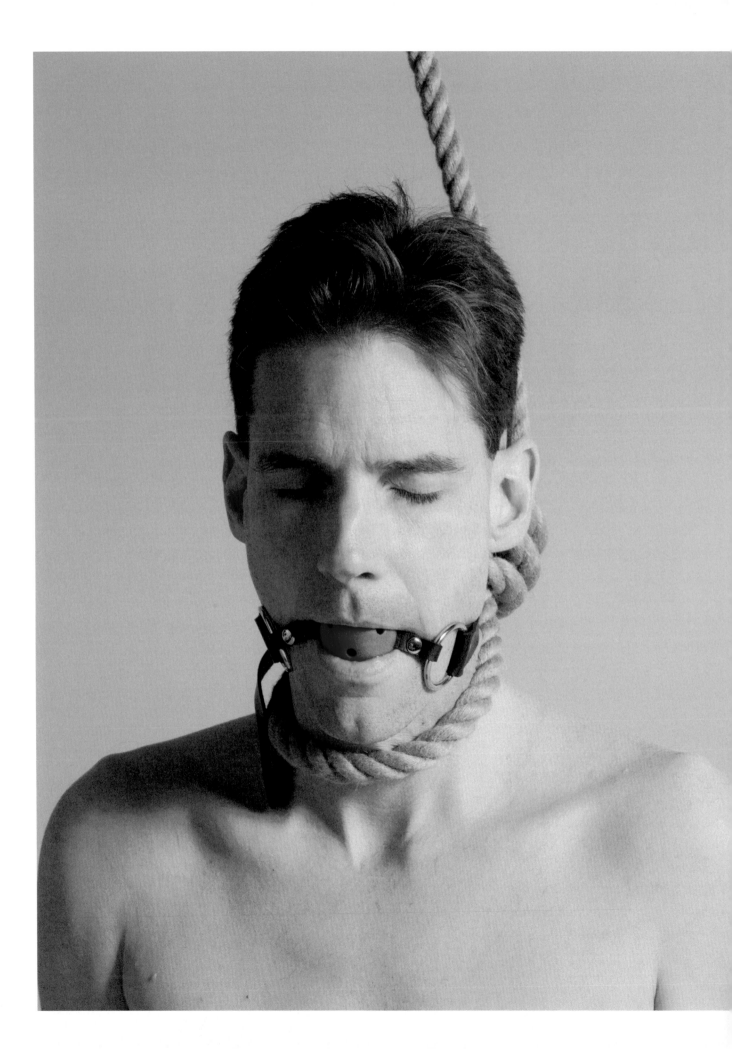

A MYTH CALLED REVERSE RACISM

I have an idea for a movie, called Pie. This film is award worthy, and sure to make the average moviegoer salivate at the mouth for its immediate release. This country loves the dystopian, fantasy, and apocalyptic genres, so hear me out. A deranged species of cold and carnivorous corpses spends thousands of years fighting in a game of thrones (no relation) for dominance of the world, where humans, deemed inferior, are forced into subservience, subjugation, and slavery. The corpses are at the top of every social, political, and economic ladder. Humans are brought up to believe that their children are expendable. The corpses sacrifice human children by ceremoniously baking them into gigantic pies and eating them for all to see. Generations of enslaved human beings are brainwashed into believing they are lesser than the corpses, who declare that their own culture, history, and ideas are righteous and superior to all others. The human beings believe it themselves, absorbing their inferiority like a jumbo tampon. The corpses demand gratitude for their wisdom and governance, claiming the human beings would have long been extinct without them. When a few humans dissent from the established world order and cry out for equality or freedom, they are called ungrateful traitors or simply murdered for having the gall to step out of line.

Eventually a brave human heroine steps in and defeats the species of corpses, though the exact type of defeat relies on the rating of the movie. Rated R and there is sure to be tons of blood and rape revenge scenes, because this is America. PG-13 begets a film with more dramatic speeches than blood. Either way, the story is neatly resolved in one to four highly profitable films and throughout the journey you get to have fan related orgasms at Comic-Con and on reddit message boards. This is one of *those* movies that inspires obsession, in the same vein as *Harry Potter*, *Lord of the Rings*, *Twilight*, and *The Hunger Games*. I can smell this movie and all the money it will generate. When not immersed in the fan culture, people can go back to their lives with little concern for the striking parallels between black people in the real world and the enslaved human beings in their favorite dystopian drama. Fans will not register that the human beings in the movie have it better than real life black Americans, as dystopian films require the inevitable victory of the protagonist and posse. Meanwhile, black Americans are now living in the fifth or sixth sequel of our journey to full racial equality, with no true ending yet in sight. The current script calls for white people to call black people racist.

It will never cease to amaze me how so many white people in this country do two things: **11** ignore the real life systems of oppression regularly depicted in film and their habit of claiming to be victims of racism. Particularly the latter, because racism is a system of political, economic, and social discriminations that affect people of color thanks to virulent white supremacy. Nobody can be racist to a white person. Racism takes place all over the world, but let's talk about here in the supposed "land of the free." You know, the place where policies that discriminate against black people have existed since before its official birth date. Before we continue down the road of open racial discussions, we must kill the notion that black people are, or ever have been, racist. We did not gain many of the same rights as white people until the 1970's, after roughly three hundred years of free labor and boosting the white ego. The exploitation, murders, and rapes of my ancestors by white people were (and still are) rarely or poorly prosecuted. We have suffered, a lot. For being black. Not for choices we made, like acquiring bad bangs or picking the wrong barber, but because of the skin color we were born into.

Though American school textbooks have been vehemently teaching that we live in a post-racial society, those of us not living in la la land know better. Many white Americans have simply traded overt and dominative racism for its covert and sneaky cousin. And yet, black people have been re-branded as the racists. We've always been considered dangerous, but now things have intensified. It's why news channels ask Karen from *Mean Girls* caliber questions like "Is Black Lives Matter a terrorist group?" It sounds deliciously dystopian and depraved- punishing the oppressed for trying to end their oppression- but this is actually real life. Black people were strung up from trees gasping for breath or screaming from roaring fires as crowds of smiling white men thanked God for the opportunity to act out his will. White people began businesses and funded associations that either exploited our labor and money or fought tirelessly to keep us from infiltrating their schools, neighborhoods, and workplaces.

To call a black person racist means you are ignoring fundamental reasons why our collective prejudice against white people exists in the first place. You're ignoring the years of violence and discrimination that makes the American pie so unique. Blacks have spent hundreds of years being the supposedly inferior subordinates of white people— and are now being told that those years have not contributed to current attitudes or social norms. Race is something white people have exploited for centuries, leading to both a blessing and curse for their descendants, who reek of various privileges but struggle to admit that the fruits of white supremacy are encrusted into each of this country's layers. Racism is the identity scourge of white people alone. Yet, so many white people get a sick thrill from accusing the people who have historically been relegated to the bottom rungs of society of being racist. They get off on accusing black people of oppressing them. A manifestation of both guilt and fetish, reverse racism is a myth.

Buyers, Not Owners

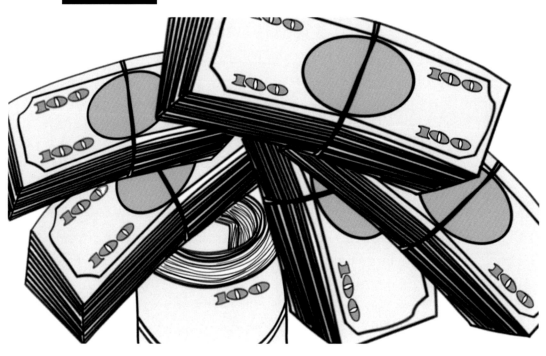

If you ask any of my closest friends they'll tell you that I aspire to buy up a swath of land in Wyoming, organize my own ranch, and sell parcels of it off to other black people who will in turn do the same. I fantasize about owning curly haired horses, cultivating a garden, building a custom house, and being surrounded by fresh air that I can puncture with the highest speeds of Wi-Fi. I will have black neighbors who will help build clinics, hair salons, barbershops, stores, charter schools, and hopefully a strip club with great wings. We'll also co-op the grocery and beauty supply stores, and there will be a small community tax that accrues college scholarship money for the children. Getting products from Asian dominated beauty supply distributors will be expensive, but because the store will be co-owned and supported by multiple wallets it will be manageable. Every building will be erected by black contractors and architects. Black-owned businesses will headquarter nearby and provide quality employment. Black children and teens will be placed in paid apprenticeships and internships in skilled trades that count for school credit. There will be a black ran police department and Wal-Mart will be a thing you randomly ventured into on a trip out of town because they simply won't exist in my utopia. The town will grow into a city eventually and be a mecca for black people.

Sigh. There I go dreaming about something that will never happen. In the present day, only 7-10% of businesses at any given time are black owned.[1] This means that on payday it doesn't take long for your hard earned dollars to leave the community. By the time you've bought your groceries, paid your bills, and bought a new outfit and hair products, your wages have made a non-black business owner wealthier. Its appalling when you consider that many of the places that cater to us- the beauty supply store, for instance- aren't owned by black people. Estimates on the total yearly dollars spent by black women on hair care exceed 500 billion bucks.[2] I'm happy that more black owned beauty supply stores are popping up than ever, but we need still need more. When we consolidate our economic power- buying and renting black or choosing the black real estate broker over the white one, for example- we will be a greater force to deal with on the American landscape. But it wont be easy. Ownership and self-reliance threatens white supremacy. Just take a look back at history. Whenever black people attempted to recycle community wealth, they were punished by angry whites who lost out on business. When the co-opted Peoples Grocery was opened by a friend of Ida B Wells (and his associates) in 1889, it flourished and became the preferred choice for shopping among black people in Memphis. This was displeasing to the owner of the nearby white grocery store, and within three years the business was destroyed and three of the co-owners had been lynched on the fallacious accusation of conspiracy. After the businesses of Black Wall Street were destroyed in 1921, white owners of competing businesses enjoyed the boost in cash that once stayed among the black Oklahoma community. Capitalism is dirty, but recycling community wealth can't be any worse than giving ALL of our money to companies that dont care about us. When black people are prosperous and spend their money with other black people who can do the same, facets of white supremacy built on black dollars begin to crumble. The large conglomerates who depend on black dollars to nourish their pockets for the lobbying of discriminatory laws will begin to crumble.

Imagine co-op grocery stores, dollar stores, and beauty supply emporiums where some of the money made is set aside for community programs, scholarships, and institutes for our children in the same manner as the Jewish community. Imagine if black clothing designers were boosted up, gassed, and supported the way foreign European brands are. My dream for a black-owned

utopia in Wyoming may never happen, but developing more black owned staple stores and products is definitely a step in the right direction. Nothing bad can come from more black ownership, but there are numerous reasons why black business endeavors fail. Racial disadvantages are at the root of the problem, but collective ignorance of the importance of community wealth recycling and financial literacy causes the cycle to continue. We can't keep ignoring the very real fact that money runs America. To fund our progression, we must fund each other.

CHRISTIANITY AND BLACK FORGIVENESS

I remember being about six or seven years old and telling a broad-chested bully at Barringer Academic Center that I forgave her constant cruelties. I proudly told her that as a child of God, I would turn my other cheek. This was after she had deliberately stepped on my foot during recess, and my outburst was a secret assertion of my exhaustion. She stepped on my foot again. My white Reeboks were trashed, and my mother was most assuredly going to kill me. "I forgive you. Jesus wants me to forgive you, I'll pray for you," I told her, hoping that she had sympathy or guilt built up in that wide body of hers. The exact linguistic response of the sadistic little brat escapes me, but I remember that the bullying did not actually stop. If anything, it worsened; I had accidentally given her the go-ahead to make me her little bitch. She was the first and last bully I ever had, but I remember her desperate desire to make me miserable as clearly as I remember the smell of the school cafeteria on fish stick day. When I told the bully that I forgave her for all past and future transgressions, she knew that she could do anything to me and that I would not put up too much of a fight. She knew that I would never stop her from bullying me, that I would only pray. I wouldn't learn for another year how to deal with bullies (it involves fists) but when I did I quickly realized that there was no room for forgiving. There was only room for fighting.

There's something soothing to white America about a crying, hurt, heavily accented black person answering post-tragedy media questions with words like *forgive* and *pray* and *Gods will*. It is a scene that has often been broadcast during the evening news or splashed across the front of newspapers, radiating trauma and pain. When Dylan Roof ruthlessly executed a church full of black people in December 2015, journalists were quick to ask victims relatives if they forgave Roof, who was nonchalantly treated to Burger King while being escorted to jail. Nobody asks the family of victims of 9/11 if they forgive Al Qaeda. Nobody shoved microphones in the faces of Sandy Hook parents or expected them to extend forgiveness to a man who murdered their children. And yet the image of the forgiving, docile, subservient black Christian has been on the American landscape for years, and has its roots in slavery.

While the relationship between black people and Christianity could fill a library, here's a quick primer. The overwhelming majority of slaves did not freely choose to become Christians. The natives of Africa had many religions, and those who made the middle passage could have observed any of them. Despite what you may have heard, there's only a small chance their religion was Christianity. Though it did exist in Ethiopia and in some parts of North Africa, Islam was the most common religion on the continent; particularly in West Africa where most slaves came from. It wasn't until the 1800s that slaves were converted to Christianity on a wide scale thanks to the Second Great Awakening, a period of time in which Americans became more religious. Some masters had a genuine belief that they had a Christian duty to civilize inferior people, including their slaves. These masters looked at indoctrinating their slaves as one of their paternalistic duties, like providing food or clothes. For others, Christianity was

15

merely a form of control. As one antebellum commentator said, "The deeper the piety of the slave, the more valuable is he in every sense of the word."[1] The value of course was a slave at peace with their status and treatment in life. As William Drayton observed in 1836, "Christianity, truly taught and sincerely cherished cannot fail to render the slave population tranquil and happy."[2]

The relationship between black people and Christianity is not completely negative. Christianity inspired Nat Turner and other slaves to rebel. The black church was an instrumental part of the Civil Rights movement. During slavery, the nadir of American race relations, and Jim Crow, Christianity provided comfort for people who had little else to hold onto. The church is still a pure beacon of hope for some in the present day. Historically black churches have been cultivating community bonds and providing aid for needy black families since the 19th century. They have been pillars of the community. Also on a more personal note, *Smile* by Kirk Franklin is a banger and I find meals on first Sunday at most black churches to be delicious. And yet, there is much to be said about a religion that has been used by white supremacists to justify black subjugation and oppression. After all, while most of us continue to pray to Jesus for equality and privileges, white supremacists have prayed to the same Jesus to maintain the status quo of white supremacy.

Currently, 78% of black Americans identify as protestant Christians. Black Christians attend religious services more frequently than their white peers and are more likely to believe in heaven.[3] Its no wonder that forgiveness and religiosity have been two themes closely acquainted with black people. Note how little black history is discussed in American history courses, except for a few familiar stories involving the anti-violent preacher man who advised prayer and kindness as a repayment to high profile murders and acts of injustice. The Christian doctrine of forgiveness has made us quick to forgive instead of reacting with vengeance, making us prime targets for control. The trope of gentle black people, guided by a strong moral compass to peacefully absolve perpetrators of white supremacy, is aided by our intense and media-caricaturized relationship with Christianity. Too many of us find comfort in praying to God to solve our problems (while also using Christian doctrine to exploit our differences and judge each other rather than come together). The byproduct of this is a heaping pile of confidence from white supremacists, who feel comfortable oppressing us because they know we won't fight back. We must stop being so forgiving. We must allow ourselves to be angry so we can channel it into change.

DIVISIONS

The Willie Lynch letter is a fake, but that doesn't mean the concept at its core wasn't accurate. The purported 18th century letter described the ways a master could turn slaves against each other for his benefit. Though proven to be fake, the letter has remained popular because of its uncanny accuracy of describing the intraracial relationships of black people. Unfortunately, many masters didn't need to be told that divided slaves were the best kind. It was just instinct. The women versus the men. The house slaves versus the field slaves. Post slavery, more divisions would pop up along the boundaries of sexuality, skin color, religion, and higher education choice. Whether divided for massas' affections, for special privileges, or for status within the community, a lot of us accept these divisions with little thought. Straight blacks torment queer blacks. Light women call dark women nasty things, claiming "issa joke". On a lesser level but still toxic level is the trend of telling super light skinned women with less kinky grades of hair that they aren't black. Christians spar with Muslims and atheists, who of course also quibble with each other. The list of opposing sides is abundant.

These divisions have been an awesome perk for white supremacists over the years. Because we're focused on seeing each other fail across various lines, we're incapable of coming together to make a progressive impact. Many of us are also incapable of empathizing with certain black identities, instead seeking to change them or erase them all together. These divisions are built from white supremacy on ideas about what blackness is, or what it should be. We judge each other on behavior that truly has no bearing on race relations and things we have no control over. We also try to restrict behavior. For example, whites called black women whores and sexually abused them for centuries… so to some black people, black women aren't allowed to exhibit consensual sexual agency in the present day because it justifies white notions of us being sexually loose. White people called black men weak and emasculated them for centuries so black men who are queer or non-masculine are apart of some conspiratorial agenda to destroy the black race. Then there's the following hotep favorite. White people didn't used to allow black people into prominent universities so black people who choose to go to them instead of HBCUs in the present day- no matter how financially lucrative or academically relevant- are self-hating traitors. These are real arguments. Ridiculous ones, but very real.

The most ridiculous one of all is the division between the black men and women. It is a division deeply rooted in each sides' refusal to acknowledge historical context. We have been coerced into clawing at each other's throats for centuries. We swallowed depictions of each other as gross stereotypes from the zip coon to the brute to the jezebel. We were bred like animals, with no regard for our personal desires in the matter. "If a hand were noted for raising up strong black bucks, bucks that would never 'let the monkey get them' while in the high-noon

17

hoeing, he would be sent out as a species of circuit-rider to the other plantations- to plantations where there was over-plus of 'worthless young nigger gals.'" recalled Georgia slave John Cole. North Carolina slave Hilliard Yellerday said "A slave girl was expected to have children as soon as she became a woman. Some of them had children at the age of twelve and thirteen years old." [1] Black women were brutalized and men were not allowed to intervene. Master's wives usually didn't intervene either, unless they wanted to brutalize the women or men themselves. Commenting on the commonality of masters having children with female slaves, Louisiana freedman Chris Franklin recalled "it seem like de white women don't mind. Dey didn't 'ject [object], 'cause dat mean more slaves." [2] As you can deduce, masters ruled over their own families and black ones thanks to patriarchy and racism. Noted by historian Peter W. Bardaglio, "They viewed female sexuality as property that they owned, like slaves, and protection of this property was a key to preserving their position in society." [3] How is this relevant?

The division between black women and men is also rooted in patriarchy. Many black men can grasp that white men have the most privileges and power in this world, but refuse to admit that it is both race AND gender that granted them all the privileges they have. Admitting that white men are powerful because of their gender requires acknowledging that some black men have re-molded white patriarchy to aid their desire of controlling black women. For example, where it used to be white men telling black women to breed to create more laborers, now it is extremist black men who say that women need to breed to bolster the population against whites. Furthermore, too many black men police the choices and lifestyles of black women, claiming to know better than them about what they want and need. White patriarchy relied on this same concept for black people overall, with masters and pro-slavery advocates often saying that we were simple creatures who would not be able to survive on our own without their careful instructions.

Another sick example of black division is the running hatred and rivalry between black Americans and black Africans. The black response to African immigrants has traditionally been negative. The term "African Booty Scratchers" was uttered across school yards galore. It reminds me of the response of Black Ohioans in the 20th century when southern negroes began moving into town. "There were no barbecue joints and storefront churches or jook joints until all these negroes came from down south… we here… are doing what we can to assimilate them."[4] Divisions in our community are clearly nothing new.

If we keep trying to create parameters of proper black identities, we'll keep squabbling amongst ourselves and losing. Instead of focusing on weeding out sell-outs, political traitors, and false prophets, too many of us are caught up placing people into categories of things we don't like. Many of us actively enjoy judging the lifestyles of people who aren't actually hurting anybody—just subverting our ideas of what blackness is. These divisions are deepened from each competing groups desire to adhere to respectability politics or maintain control over the black identity. Each group wants to be the right one, policing the other by dictating what is authentic blackness and what is the result of white brainwashing. These divisions among sexuality, religion, gender, and alumni affiliation serve little purpose in dismantling white supremacy because we are all black. Read the last part of the previous sentence again if you need to. These divisions encourage violence, hatred, and apathy in addition to making our population easier to exploit. Easier to oppress. We all have different experiences with the various facets of oppression, which leads to even more divisions. While we can't change or erase these divisions overnight we can try harder to understand why they exist to increase empathy towards each other. Empathy will then erase those lines that have largely been drawn for us. You fear what you don't understand. You hate what you fear.

ENTERTAINERS, ATHLETES, AND US

If you ask the average black person to list ten black scientists, engineers, lawyers, and doctors, their answer is likely to disappoint you. They'll cobble off the obvious ones- Johnny Cochran and Neil deGrasse Tyson, maybe George Washington Carver or Dr. Daniel Hale Williams. To fill the quota, they might throw in Ben Carson. But if you ask that same person to name black athletes and entertainers, they'll mentally flip through a gargantuan directory of names before rattling off a list of favorites. Thanks to American celebrity culture that grants extreme wealth and visibility, black entertainers and athletes arguably hold more weight than anyone in black communities except Jesus Christ and Barack Obama. They are commonly from low income or middle class black families, bolstering community pride and encouraging crippling idolization that makes them immune to criticism or accountability. While white intellectuals have received accolades and fame for the greater part of American history, the accomplishments of their black counterparts have often been diminished in favor of highlighting black entertainers and athletes. This has only made black entertainers and athletes more important.

The legacy of entertainers and athletes stretches back to the antebellum days, when slaves with musical talent or exceptional labor were singled out and sometimes rewarded with special treatment. Because musicians were revered for their entertainment value by both masters and their fellow slaves, special treatment could involve clothes, food, pocket change, and less supervision.

After slavery scores of black Americans lived a terrified existence under Jim Crow well into the 1960s. While black athletes and celebrities lived with more privileges, they were not free from racism. In addition to being barred from most professional sports teams until 1946, most black athletes experienced racialized accusations of being unfairly biologically advantaged or were targeted by the press when they beat white opponents. Wrote one frustrated black writer in 1923,

"When a Black man wins a big victory in the ring, some of the big writers compare him with an African gorilla and cartoon him as the most terrible beast in the jungles – an unfair picture and comparison."[1]

Black athletes were also swindled and controlled. Boxer Joe Louis, whose white handlers gobbled up the majority of the four million dollars he made during his fifteen-year career, was not allowed to be photographed with white women or be cocky about his wins. Later celebrities like Josephine Baker, Dorothy Dandridge, Paul Robeson, and Harry Belafonte appeared to live wealthy and luxurious lifestyles, but often faced similar challenges of racism behind the scenes. Regardless, the publicized images and exploits of both athletes and celebrities were intriguing to black Americans. Celebrity gossip in the black press became prominent from 1919 onward. Some readers were charmed by celebrity pulchritude, others were aroused by their wealth, but many were enraptured by the other benefits celebrities appeared to have. On top of fame and jet setting, they were granted access to exclusive social and political circles that no other black people were allowed in. But more than anything, black athletes and celebrities were a source of pride for many. When they won, we all won. "Negroes everywhere in America…must contemplate  with deep satisfaction and pride the athletic prowess of Jesse Owens." reported the Atlanta Daily World in 1935.[2]

Celebrity culture has intoxicated most Americans since the early 20th century, but it sits on a higher pedestal in black communities. Entertainment and athletics were the two arenas that black people were allowed into if they had enough talent. Unfortunately, black intellectuals have never gotten as much shine as their white counterparts nor their entertaining black peers. Becoming a lawyer, doctor, engineer, or scientist while black was much more difficult because raw talent was not enough. Those lanes required college admission, tuition, and accreditation from racist entities for practice. The few blacks who did manage to make it into those fields were often not celebrated or accepted by mainstream America (or by their own communities) because they were overshadowed by white people. While white innovators have been heralded from the pages of textbooks for the entirety of formalized education, many of the accomplishments and contributions of black intellectuals and professionals have been sanitized and quietly written about over the past two centuries. Some are rarely mentioned, if at all.

Black intellectuals and professionals have historically been denied access to the spaces that would have allowed them to truly flex on everybody. They got into fewer schools, got less research money, and got less opportunities to showcase their skills. White American children are groomed to know that they can be anything and that their dreams are not limited to basketball player or rapper. They are bombarded with heroes who look like them from the athletic, entertainment, and intellectual realms while black people cannot say the same. Entertainers and athletes exist as successful symbols of black Americans who managed to conquer the treacherous battlefield of capitalism and racism. Being rich and gaining admittance to the highest rungs of white society like black celebrities was and continues to be a fantasy for many black folks. The love for black athletes and entertainers increased during the second half of the 20th century, when the NBA, NFL, and rap music genre became popular. In the present day 67% of NFL players and 76% of NBA players are black. These careers average 1.5 million and 6 million a year respectively. The rap industry, largely dominated by black performers, rakes in over 10 billion dollars a year.[3] The most famous black rappers, singers, and actors make mil-

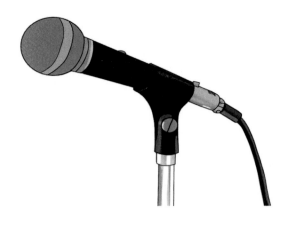

lions of dollars a year and rack up an infinite number of press engagements. In a country that never wanted black people to succeed, black celebs and athletes are iconic.

Icon status comes with some drawbacks and responsibilities though. though. There are a number of areas in which black celebs escape true critique from the masses. Take black rappers and their highly intoxicating lifestyles of greed and materialism. "Black rappers do not owe the black community anything" is an attitude often regurgitated when someone critiques a prominent recording artists' publicized efforts of philanthropy. On twitter I decided to do an experiment. I posted pictures of prominent rappers donating money to schools. In one picture a rapper donated a million while wearing no jewels and a hoodie. The other picture was of a group of three wrappers wearing head to toe designer and gold jewelry donating $1000 to a school. I asked; Couldn't that jewel draped rap group have donated more than $1000 dollars to the school? To too many, "They didn't have to donate *anything.*" was the applauded clap back. "You don't know how much money they make." was another response that made me point out how often they brag about how much money they make in their music. One helpful follower even posted a link to an article about the rap groups' net worth to back me up. I then recalled the many videos and pictures of them showing off money and expensive luxury goods that exist on the internet. "Well how much money did YOU donate?" was the last resort response from angry fans. I easily pointed out that I'm not wealthy, nor am I a rapper who regularly talks about how much money I make and spend.

The true issue is not how much the rappers donated. I wanted people to notice the money wrapped around their necks, the money in the music videos and Instagram clips- compared to the money on the giant check. Promoting excessive materialism in the community is common in rap music, so much that it eclipses giving back and efforts of community unity. Nobody expects black people with money to fork it over to the masses. Just like white entertainers, black entertainers don't owe the black community anything- but if they rely on the support of said community to get them where they are, or expect black people to rally behind them when they've been mistreated professionally, they do need to be helping out a little harder. Before rappers go mainstream, reaching out to where those hungry white dollars are, who bumps their stuff in the hood, at the strip clubs, and talks about them in podcasts and on black Twitter? Whoops, I think I gave away the answer there. WE are there for them. WE put them on. WE go after media outlets and production companies when they've been discriminated against or mistreated. When they get skimmed over for awards, unfairly attacked by their respective industries, or get in to trouble with the law, who comes rushing to their aid? More often than not it is their black fans, who admire them and want to protect their success in the face of racism.

A portion of amazing black celebs and athletes do what they can, but not enough really go above and beyond to make a difference. Despite the existence of black intellectuals and professionals, the visibility of black entertainers and athletes (and the special status they hold in the community) gives them a non-negotiable duty, especially if they rely on us. After all, when they win, we win. At least, thats how it works for most of us. This is clearly evident by the go to defense of "They just want to put a black man down," whenever a male celebrity is met with valid criticism of their misogynistic behavior, criminal activity, or lack of philanthropy. People give them no accountability. Time after time, numerous black celebrities have let the community down after collecting our career-building co-signs, cash, and defense from scandals.

Before you think I'm being unfair, I do realize that industry backlash and blackballing is a very real possibility for entertainers and athletes who challenge the status quo too harshly. History is dotted with black figures who spoke out against racism and were punished for it. Paul Robeson, who was a prominent singer and actor while simultaneously being an outspoken critic of American racism and capitalism, was blacklisted by the entertainment industry and banned by the government from receiving a passport until 1958. The reason why? According to the state department, "His frequent criticism of the treatment of blacks in the United States should not be aired in foreign countries."[4] The extent of the government's sense of pettiness with Robeson knew no bounds. A 1950's comprehensive book on American football failed to list the former Rutgers player or his status as an All-American. Josephine Baker, who once staged a citizen's arrest of a derogatory white person in California, was also harassed by the American government for her anti-racism remarks. She found refuge in Paris, where she was treated with more respect. In a more recent sense, think about Colin Kaepernick, who decided to kneel during the national anthem to recognize the importance of black lives and has been crucified by white America.

While I freely admit that speaking up about black issues can harm entertainers and athletes' careers, I do think that giving passes to the ones who do absolutely nothing for the community is for the birds. We criticize their skills and creations but rarely question their roles in our oppression. The materialism, megalomania, and misogyny. The silence on social issues and complete disinterest in amplifying black voices calling out from poverty and pain. Not all entertainers and athletes only passionately claim their blackness for press or award show re-dos, but too many do. They know they can filch the larger portion of the black communities' love, support, and money no matter how many times they leave us hanging.

But the quagmire of black entertainers and athletes is much deeper than the creation of a group of supreme black folk who inspire wealth envy and poor financial choices in grown adults. The idolization of black entertainers and athletes also instills illogical hopes of wealth and fame in our children. In a country where 6% of all STEM professionals, 4% of all physicians, and less than 5% of lawyers are black, 53% of black high school males hope for a career in sports or entertainment.[5] Why is it that so many black kids, when compared to their peers, limit their aspirations to entertainment and athletics? Because we have been socialized into believing these are the only realms that black people (particularly black males) can be successful in. Unfortunately, we stop conversations about how black athletes and entertainers function not only as inspirational stories but also as bad influences on the basis of "black people always hating." **23**

FINANCIAL DISADVANTAGES

Black people hate talking about money, unless we're talking about spending it. Even hinting at telling someone that they're financially irresponsible will gain you a rebuke mightier than a preacher driving out demons. Like most people, black Americans don't like to feel stupid. Conversations about money make many of us uncomfortable, especially when unfamiliar terms more complex than *savings account* get thrown into the mix. But there is a serious problem between green and black in the red, white, and, blue. What exactly does roughly 400 years of forced unpaid labor, unfair pay, disproportionately high interest loans, and frequent loan and mortgage denials have to do with the pockets of modern day black folks? If you were to judge the state of black wealth and financial stability from what you see on social media, in music videos, and in tabloid reports about which rapper just bought what, things would look pretty dope.

It's a vicious mirage, however. According to *Forbes*, the typical black household has 6% of the wealth of the typical white household. The wealth gap between white and black Americans has tripled since 1984, from $85,000 to $236,500 in 2009. The typical white family makes roughly $50,000 a year, while the typical black family earns $32,000.[1] While many black people have climbed out of dirt poor poverty the majority of our 19th and 20th century counterparts suffered through, too many remain stuck to the very bottom. Thirty-nine percent of black children live in poverty. Thity-seven percent of black people are homeless.[2] These people are the unfortunate pawns of a cycle built on institutional racism designed to stifle generational wealth and provide a never-ending stream of cheap laborers. While the lower class is composed of entirely too many black Americans, the richest and most influential upper class is composed of entirely too many white Americans. The court is tilted in their favor, giving them social and political advantages over the few blacks who manage to breach their brackets. Parents in this upper class have money and knowledge to bestow on their children, enough to give them a headstart that requires less labor and hardships. Meanwhile, black people in the hood are groomed for low paying jobs in retail or fast food. They are frequent targets of scheming check cashing places with high interest payday loans. Seventeen percent of blacks, compared to five percent of whites, use loan sharks, pawn shops, and payday loans to supplement their income.[3] Many of these same people send their children to crappy schools where personal finance courses aren't a requirement (but gym is)… which means students learn their money habits at home. All the while they and their parents are bombarded with American materialism values, usually finding themselves in appalling debt because they never learned how to save and invest, just spend. To make things worse, studies show that attending college, working full time, and spending less does not close the racial gap. Any reasonable person must ask why this is.

Before 1865, about ten percent of blacks were free. These lucky few had run away or were set free by generous masters; some were even bequeathed with funds. They were lucky because they had the opportunity to work for pay (no matter how paltry), while slaves worked for free. This 10%

had an early crack at accumulating wealth, while the remaining 90% were set free from bondage with dust in their pockets and little to no knowledge about finances. Most probably had no inkling that their labor had built multimillion dollar companies, aided universities, funded inheritances, and sustained cities on both sides of the Mason Dixon Line. Some enrolled in Freedman Bureau built schools and went onto become teachers or college graduates. Some went on to start businesses, but that was always a risky endeavor when prosperity could draw the lynch inducing envy of a local white man. Black businesses were routinely destroyed during riots and KKK night rides, effectively discouraging most black Americans from setting up shop during the Nadir of American Race Relations. Some blacks scraped out livings as entertainers. But the majority of freed people instead went into exploitative fields like sharecropping, railroad building, and domestic work. They were often illiterate.

Keeping all of that in mind, there were some glaring factors that put widespread black financial progress and generational wealth into a stranglehold. For one, it was highly uncommon for black laborers to get equal pay as whites. This is still reflected in 2017. On average black men earn 73 percent of what white men make, and black women earn even less than both groups. Financial disadvantages were also exacerbated by the prevalence of housing discrimination, which put a strain on already tight resources. Black business owners were routinely denied loans, causing a higher rate of failure in black entrepreneurship. Lastly, white flight into suburbia during the 1950s and deindustrialization in the 1970s led to extreme urban decay in once thriving cities like Youngstown, Detroit, Baltimore, Cleveland, and Chicago. Many of these cities had large black populations who were hit especially hard by pay cuts and layoffs. Completing this ugly illustration is the reality that many black Americans fashioned their money habits after their financially illiterate parents and ancestors. Schools are required to teach you about quadratics and photosynthesis in preparation for you being a well-rounded and adult American citizen, but somehow personal finance courses are elective options not taught everywhere. It's almost as if being financially responsible isn't encouraged.

Feel free to interrupt me here and point out that things have since changed; that figures like Oprah, Diddy, and Floyd Mayweather are irrefutable proof of black financial excellence. But that's not accurate when you consider the twenty-eight percent of black people (about 10.9 million of us) living below the poverty line.[4] Even more live barely above it, working paycheck to paycheck to live slightly better than their parents. The cycle is a dreary one. Mix in exploitative slave labor in the exponentially growing food and retail industries, the prison industrial complex, and a widening wealth gap between white and black Americans. It is clear that financial disadvantages are a key component of black oppression. Even clearer? Financial literacy and community wealth recycling are key components of dismantling it.

GO BACK TO AFRICA, NIGGER!

My junior year of college a friend convinced me to download an app called Yik Yak. She was the same friend who had introduced me to Snapchat, so I trusted her judgment. Unfortunately, Yik Yak was a septic tank of racism and bigotry. It was even worse than Twitter, because it was limited to people in my immediate area and all postings were anonymous. In case you're unfamiliar with the app, people could vote posts up or down similar to reddit. The masochistic half of me checked the app periodically, but I wasn't truly appalled by anything posted there until November 2014. After the death of 12-year-old Tamir Rice, a collective of black students (informally and cleverly called Black OSU) held a prayer circle in the Ohio State University student union. Going to a predominately white university was extremely tense and nerve-wracking for a lot of black people during that time, including myself. By no means am I religious, but the death of Tamir shook me to my core. I felt lonely and afraid, a feeling I hadn't felt since my second year of high school. I needed to be around people who understood what I was feeling. So I went to the prayer circle and held hands with folks that I normally only saw at parties or the club. There were people I didn't know and people I didn't like, but in that moment I felt intimately close to all of them. There were about 300 of us crowded into a misshapen circle holding hands, and the feeling it gave me is hard to put into words. I cried. I trembled. I felt hopeful. I saw the annoyed and confused white faces walk by the prayer circle, but I focused instead on the faces of men and women who cared that a 12-year-old had been unjustly murdered just a few hundred miles away in Cleveland. I heard a few snickers but there was no direct dissent from white passerby. But later that night on Yik Yak, between sex updates and song lyrics, I saw their real feelings bubble to the surface.

First, "Seeing all those monkeys in the union made my skin crawl. Affirmative action, much?!" Then, "They'll gather for a thug but I bet none of those coons ever went to a memorial service for VETERANS." There were a few variations of "I hate niggers." But the most popular yak of all was "If you don't like America, go back to AFRICA!"

It shouldn't have been a surprise. Telling black people to go back to Africa has been a common response to our trauma and pain for nearly two centuries now. After the conclusion of the Civil War and during the throes of reconstruction, many white Americans wanted to return their heavily used merchandise back to the shelf. This idea had been popular before and during the war, as well. Said Abraham Lincoln in 1854, "If all earthly power were given to me, my first impulse would be to free all the slaves and send them to Liberia to their own native land." Many slave owners wanted free blacks to leave so that they wouldn't taint the minds of their slaves. In addition to white supporters, there was a population of free blacks that wanted to leave America, and their combined desires catalyzed the back to Africa movement that originally gained traction in the early 19th century. From 1822 to 1867, roughly 13,000 black people were shipped to Liberia through the American Colonization Society. However, this effort was largely a failure because the majority of black people stayed in America out of financial reluctance or plain inclination, even after slavery. Still, "Go Back to Africa" is a phrase hurled by racists at black Americans when they complain about inequality or race relations. The phrase is packed with animosity and hatred.

America is not your home. You're not an American. You would not be missed if you ever left. This is a place where we have reluctantly given you privileges that you were never supposed to have, and by acting ungrateful you are reminding me how much I really don't want you and your people here. You are burdens.

Most rights that black people have were only extended to us after perilous political and social fights that involved violence. None of the rights we wrestled away came without spilling copious amounts of blood. For freedom, for voting rights, for desegregation, and for legitimate interest in our causes. If we never had fought for the things we wanted, we never would have gotten them. Generations of white Americans have been complicit with the status quo. For every white outspoken critic of Jim Crow race relations or every white volunteer during the Civil Rights Movement, there was a comfortable and privileged group of white people saying "What do these black people want now? They're not slaves anymore!" These types of white people are not extinct, even though they should be. Their reluctance to extend to black people the full range of privileges that white people enjoy is proof that we are not considered real citizens.

My classmates on Yik Yak spoke with the freedom that anonymity grants. They didn't make suggestions like "Go Back to Africa" when I spoke in class (save for one moron in a sociology course who obviously hadn't done that week's assigned readings). But the sentiment is strong in White America. A quick Google search of "Go Back to Africa" on google will reveal that fact to you. The feelings behind this popular quip are oppressive. Our skin color has impacted our ability to be regarded as full American citizens. Irish and Italian Americans faced discrimination, but skin color allowed them to assimilate in a way impossible to black Americans. Remember that we are differentiated as "African Americans." White Americans are simply called Americans. When they complain, they are not told to go back to Ireland, Italy, Britain, or Germany. Because they are actual Americans; their concerns are legitimate. But when *African Americans* complain? We are ignored and told we can just take our ungrateful asses back to Africa.

HOUSING WOES

1958 Chicago. You and your partner want to buy a house for the family. You currently live in what is known as the black belt, in a cramped studio apartment built for two with an actual population of six. You're optimistic about buying a home because neighborhood covenants that barred black people from moving in were outlawed ten years ago. You and your partner go to the bank and apply for a loan. You both have decent jobs, decent savings, and decent credit, but get denied. Frustrated, it seems like you won't be getting a house anytime soon. Then from a friend of a friend, you hear about a self-proclaimed pro-black real estate broker who helps unfortunate couples get good homes with low money down. Three weeks later you and your family have a beautiful house of your own. You have plans to decorate and enjoy it. You have no idea that a white family recently vacated the home and sold it for roughly $12,000; but you do know that you owe $26,000 to your landlord before the place is officially yours. It's not long before you begin noticing that your beautiful house has some serious problems; leaky pipes or rodent infestations. When you bring it up to the landlord, he tells you that these things are building violations and that he must fine you for immediate repairs. This throws your family's tight budget for a loop, so you and your partner both get second jobs. After all, if you miss one house payment, your home will be repossessed.

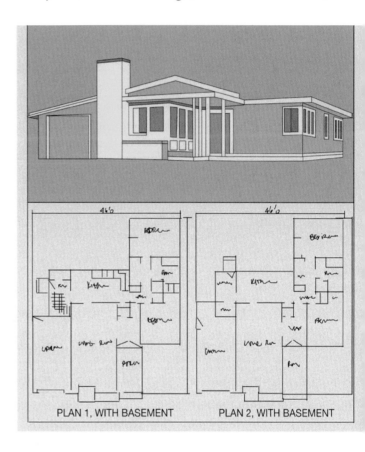

Before you know it, it's been three years. The house is still not yours. You've stopped seeing your kids as much as you used to. You're constantly irritable or unavailable for their attention. You have less time for discipline and barely remember the last time you spoke to a teacher at their school. You do know that they go to class in the afternoon and come home at night because their school is bursting at the seams with students. To cope, the school pulls double shifts. As for you, you have no social life or hobbies because you're constantly at work. You and your partner rarely see each other in non-bedroom settings. But no matter how many hours you work and pennies you pinch, one month you and your partner realize your wallets are about $200 short for rent. Three and a half years in and your home has accrued zero equity and both of your accounts are tapped dry. By the next month your beautiful dream home has been repossessed and you and your family are now penniless and crawling to the hood for public housing.

This was the reality for many black families in Chicago, who were dual victims of blockbusting and contract buying. Because many were denied loans and mortgages thanks to the Federal Housing Act, their options for attaining homes were few. People were crammed into kitchenette and basement apartments with no plumbing and rampant disease. Said one housing administrator in 1958, "We don't try to enforce the overcrowding provisions in the housing code too strongly in negro neighborhoods. After all, where would the people go? We'd have at least 75,000 out on the streets."[1] The southernmost area of the black belt was reserved for black elites and other parts of the city were for closely knitted white ethnic groups, effectively relegating low income blacks to the overcrowded slums. If a family tried to get out, they found themselves in the unscrupulous world of contract sellers, who also doubled as blockbusters. The scam was quite simple. Speculators would scare an all white area into selling their homes for cheap, on the notion that niggers were invading their neighborhoods. Tactics to stir up fear involved paying black men to fight in the streets and hiring black mothers to take leisurely walks down sidewalks with strollers. When the first white family inevitably fled for the suburbs for a hastily negotiated low profit, the contract seller then took the home and sold it to a black family at a high markup. This caused a chain reaction among neighbors, until entire blocks of Chicago were busted. While contract buying and block busting didn't happen everywhere like it did in Chicago, cities across the country experienced redlining from 1934 until the late 1960s. The Federal Housing Administration advised banks to avoid giving loans to people living in areas with undesirable racial groups. This set the foundation for ghettoization, which trapped millions of blacks in cycles of disadvantage and isolation. When the Chicago Housing Authority sought to ease the congestion of the black belt and build public housing in less crowded areas, white people were pissed. Facing backlash, the CHA erected public housing in the ghetto to keep black residents contained and away from white neighborhoods. Low or nonexistent loan approval rates in these areas meant fewer business ventures, which in turn meant fewer jobs. Overcrowding and low property values meant inferior schools and less community resources. From desperation and lack of opportunities came crime, which flourished. Cops were negligent or corrupt. As all of these components converged, white Americans voiced their disgust with how black people degraded themselves and their neighborhoods. Primetime news exposés on the state of black ghettos reached a fever pitch during the 60s and 70s. Blame was placed on broken families, crime, and laziness… but not on housing discrimination, school funding, or financial disadvantages.

This mirrors modern conversations about the violent hoods of Chicago, Baltimore, St Louis, Detroit, and similar places that are rooted in racism. People criticize and demonize the people in these cities without understanding the full picture. Racism set these populations up for failure. In 1968, the Fair Housing Act was passed in a half-ass effort to end redlining. Discriminatory practices have not gone away in the present day, though. Black people continue to be the targets of unfair practices, like higher loans. Between 2004 and 2006, Chicago was the American city with the most residents holding subprime loans.[2] It was recently revealed that in the 2000s Wells Fargo was pushing pricey subprime loans to black people in churches, which were referred to as "ghetto loans" in the company's internal memos.[3]

IDENTITY THEFT

I was in enrolled in elementary school the first time I was called an "Oreo". For those of you not privy to cruel grade school slang, someone deemed an Oreo is considered to be black on the outside but white on the inside. My English was too proper and my voracious interest in reading somehow signaled to my that I was "trying to be white." I didn't realize it at the time, but the people who told me this were perpetuating an antiquated shard of white supremacy: that whiteness and intelligence are mutually exclusive.

My earliest memories of being told I was smart are also at my elementary school, where second graders were tested for gifted abilities and separated into tribes that lasted for the next three years. Barringer was a Charlotte school touted for its revolutionary diversity. It was filled with poor black kids who lived around the school, and upper class and middle class white kids were imported from nicer areas of town. There were three levels— Horizons, Talent Development, and Learning Immersion. Horizons was for the geniuses, TD was for the gifted kids, and LI was for the 'normal' kids. There were less than a dozen black children sitting with me in my gifted "talent development" classes. It was like we were in an exclusive club. The white kids talked to us instead of looking through us. I was often told how "smart" and "articulate" I was by incredulous parents of my white peers during weekend sleepovers and after school Odyssey of the Mind meetings. It was something I began to relish after a while. The kids and teachers alike looked down on the students in the "Learning Immersion" program, who were all black and Latino save for one white student. In their classes, they weren't called gifted or talented. They were the same kids who called me an Oreo.

The term "social death" describes the dehumanizing experience of an African during the transatlantic slave trade. Africans were snatched from their cultures, where people who looked like them filled various roles and statuses. They weren't all kings and queens; an inspiring yet erroneous idea peddled by black supremacists to demonstrate our divinity. The indigenous people of Africa had robust communities and hierarchies, but everybody who looked like us was not forced to be at the bottom, like they were in America, where "slave" was the predominant identity. In America, their native traditions, languages, religions, and social habits were replaced with European ones. Free blacks existed, but they were not fully esteemed American citizens and they were expected to assimilate to American ways of life or face punishment.

The entire time this was happening, white people deluded themselves into opulent superiority complexes kept in place by lies and violence. While white people praised their own physical features, they denounced black ones. They promoted the myth that slaves who wished to be free were psychologically crazy. They perpetuated the concept of the idiotic coon, while also not allowing slaves to read and write test their theory of inferior intelligence. They called us pathetic and naturally subservient creatures who couldn't survive on our own. For centuries white people told black people they were inferior in virtually every realm except physical strength and athletics. Whites were prettier, smarter, more advanced, and worthier of rights and respect. Pushing back against these notions usually ended in misery, but many blacks tried anyways. Blacks learned to read and write in secret, ran away, and a handful attempted to orchestrate vio- **31** lent rebellions. However, most slaves didn't push back because they were brainwashed into their inferior positions and didn't even know rebellion was a possibility. They had been molded into the perfect inferiors.

When the first slaves arrived in America from Africa, they still had a connection to home— where people who looked like them were more than slaves and second class citizens. Black people were kings and queens, warriors, merchants, and hunters; they were autonomous beings. This connection to the past was beaten out of most of the slaves, or died with them when their children were born blank slates and indoctrinated into inferiority. Their identities were created for them by white people, who had no interest in grooming their self-esteem. When slavery ended, the identity crisis continued. We were torpedoed as insatiable rapists, lazy government leeches, ugly creatures, violent thugs, deadbeat fathers, bitter black women, and sexual deviants— all stereotypes born from racial discrimination and slavery. If black people were praised, it was because they held some form of value. You know, like the athletes and entertainers.

Black people were also regularly called intellectually inferior, as dictated by eugenicists and scientific racists. Twentieth century radio, television, and film pulsated with these parameters of the black identity, particularly ideas about our inferior intelligence. When a black intellectual dared to exist, he or she was often discredited or handled with deeply rooted feelings of disbelief. Take 12-year-old Gloria Lockerman, who spelled "antidisestablishmentarianism" on the 1955 quiz show "The 64,000 Dollar Question". The intelligence she exhibited was not something associated with black people; and newspapers made sure to divulge that she was black when reporting on her feat. Her intelligence wasn't the focus. Her skin was.

Blackness was, and often still is, associated with intellectual inferiority by both white and black Americans. Its why childhood peers associated intellectuality with whiteness and why various white adults gushed over how articulate I was as a child. It's why so many black children aspire to have careers in entertainment and athletics over intellectual fields. For too long the black identity has been molded by white society and what they think blackness is. We're more sexually experienced than white people, black fathers are deadbeats, and black women have big butts. These generalizations influence us. It's why so many black men measure the extent of their manhood using the quantity of their sexual conquests. It's why a white racist will ask a black person if they know their father. Its why so many black women with flat asses or non-existent hips feel "less authentic".

For too long, a manufactured, generic, and widely accepted version of the black identity has boxed a significant portion of our population into dissatisfaction, self-hatred, or mediocrity. Too many black people since 1865 have subconsciously limited views of what blackness is, just like our antebellum ancestors, who only knew slavery and the ironically named free blacks. Very few knew blacks to be wealthy, intellectual, political, or in charge of their own affairs. If they did know these kinds of blacks, they were the snooty and non-encouraging kind, who didn't want competition or overshadowing from their own. The passage of time has broadened the spectrum of the black identity, but the internalized inferiority complex brought about by American slavery has not completely dissolved in the present day.

I often think about the kids who called me an Oreo during grade school. I wasn't called an Oreo in my high school years, but I was surrounded by peers who doubted their own abilities. Most of the teachers had given up on trying with them long ago, and they were rarely told that they had any intellectual gifts. They were the same ones who thought it was "lame" to read or enjoy intellectual pursuits. Did they ever grow out of equating intelligence with whiteness? If they didn't, for most of them, did maintaining the black identity of willful ignorance hold them back from reaching their full potential? According to my recent scouring of Facebook, the answer is an unfortunate yes.

JUSTICE SYSTEM BLUES

Have you ever really sat back and thought about what freedom is? The word has been tossed around by various groups of people since this country was first established. Defined, freedom is the power or right to act, speak, or think as one wants without hindrance or restraint. Unfortunately, when the American forefathers won freedom in 1776, this privilege wasn't for everyone. "No refuge could save the hireling and slave, From the terror of flight or the gloom of the grave, And the star-spangled banner in triumph doth wave, O'er the land of the free and the home of the brave." This is the third verse of the Star Spangled Banner. When the slaves were released from bondage, there was both joy and confusion. "I was free three years before I knowed it. Worked along just de same. One day we was in de field… man come along on big, black horse… stopped, waved his hands and shouted, "you is free, all of you. Go anywhere you wants to." Us quit right then and acted de fool," recalled a South Carolina slave.[1] But the joy was short-lived, because again freedom was not for everybody. Mississippi didn't ratify the thirteenth amendment until 2013. Some states stalled on ratifying the 14th amendment to turn black people into citizens, like my home state of North Carolina, which waited two whole years. Kentucky didn't

even bother to ratify the fourteenth amendment until 1976.

When rumors circulated that freed people would get forty acres and a mule as post-slavery reparations, some blacks refused to sign work contracts so they could claim their prizes. This pissed off and terrified southern whites, who heard another rumor that blacks would rebel if they didn't get their land. By the end of 1865, southern states were whipping up black codes. These codes were modeled after antebellum era free black and slave codes that were created to keep the two groups from mingling or stepping outside of their respective statuses. Slave owners and other whites alike were terrified of slave insurrection. After the Civil War tore through the South and decimated family and state fortunes grown from the seeds of slave labor, fear festered along with anger. During the reconstruction years, this fear was based on the thought of negro-delivered retribution and the alleged danger of black idleness and vagrancy. The terror and anger was compounded by labor shortages from newly freed blacks who desired less work and more leisure time. Black code violations included public drunkenness and moving through the wrong part of town at the wrong time of day. In South Carolina, black people could not fill positions other than farmers or servants without an annual license from a judge. Some states required that black orphans be forced into labor. Others passed laws banning black people from arming themselves. Nine states, including Louisiana and Tennessee, developed vagrancy laws to create profitable forced labor groups. An 1882 Kentucky newspaper listed a "likely negro vagrant" being sold at Lexington for $31.[2] The sale was a one-year labor contract. In Louisiana, every black person had to be employed by a white person who was in charge of their conduct. It was slavery all over again.

Men in eight of the states with vagrancy laws who were unlucky enough to be out of work or self-employed were arrested and thrown into the exploitative world of convict leasing. Men who were arrested for other crimes weren't immune either. If they had a trial at all, they faced all white juries who promptly found them guilty. Black on white crime received harsher sentences than any other demographic pairing. After being stripped of what little freedom they had, these men were shipped off to small camps and rented out like mules by the state for neat profits. As you can guess this quickly became a driving force in arresting black people. Also, most southern states didn't have the desire or money to provide around the clock care and supervision for prisoners. Labor was a productive way to kill time.

It is an incredibly similar tale today. In the land of the free, thirty nine percent of the people in prison are black, despite us being only thirteen percent of the population.[3] Black people are still being targeted for silly and racialized laws. For example, numerous studies have shown black people are between two and five times more likely than whites to be arrested for weed possession. According to the American Civil Liberties Union, black on white crime is still punished more harshly than white on black crime. Juries are predominately white… when trials actually take place. Many offenders are swindled into plea deals.[4] A study in New York found that black defendants are more likely to be offered plea deals that include jail time than their white peers. University of Pennsylvania law professor David S Abrams found that judges show **35** racial bias when sentencing. When facing judges considered the least affected by racial bias, black people are thirty percent more likely to end up in jail than whites. When facing judges that are more affected by racial bias, that percentage doubles.[5]

Former convict leasing state Louisiana currently holds the precious rank of highest incarceration rate in the world, and the most inmates in private prisons.[6] Speaking of private prisons, there are thirty-three states that currently have them. These states have adopted the same attitude about correctional facilities as the 19th century jerks who utilized convict leasing. Their focus is on profits, stripping away developmental programs in favor of low paying production jobs is a win-win. The government gives private prisons a certain amount of money per prisoner, and the prison then does all it can to keep expenditures low so that profits remain high. Profits are also the goals of government ran prisons, as well. Unicor, a government entity once known as the "Federal Prison Industries", pays its incarcerated employees between 23 cents to $1.15 an hour to produce things like the protective gear worn by the military.

The growth of private prisons accelerated thanks to the preposterous War on Drugs, initiated by Ronald Reagan two years before crack was officially an epidemic. Like black codes over a century before, drug laws passed during this time were for thugs and fiends, carefully coded language for black people. Harsh sentencing laws allowed higher minimum sentences for crack related offenses over cocaine related ones. While cocaine was more expensive and used by whites, crack was not only cheap and accessible for disadvantaged black folk but racialized by the news and politicians as a predominantly black problem, despite its high use by white Americans. The mass incarceration of black people continued during the Bush, Clinton, Bush Jr, and Obama administrations.

The meaning of freedom was set on fire somewhere along the line for the sake of keeping white Americans safe and comfortable- as well as keeping money pumping through the economy. After all, the war on drugs is very lucrative for state and local law enforcement. The Washington Post reported that federal authorities seized more than $5 billion in 2014 for their forfeiture fund and that, from 2001 to 2014, police had seized $2.5 billion in cash without warrants or indictments.[7] In addition to the privilege of keeping and using seized property and assets, drug task forces are given Byrne grants, which are "spent on everything from military grade hardware to officer overtime."[8] Numerous former cops have attested to the fact that they while on duty they were encouraged to go out and arrest as many people as possible to stay on top of quotas and receive federal money.

Despite these head spinning realities that make America's justice system one of the largest among developed nations, contrarians will bark that everyone in prison is there for a good reason. They claim that black men disproportionately making up a chunk of the inmate population is due to their criminal nature, disregarding any criminal factors. "I'm not a racist," they say. "But your people are just prone to crime and violence." They ignore the fact that racial profiling means black people are more subject to stop and frisks and being pulled over. Because white

people are less likely to get profiled for crimes, they're less likely to be caught doing them. Take this shocking example in Volusia County, Florida. A reporter found that in 148 hours of video footage and over 1000 traffic stops, eighty percent of the people stopped were blacks and Latinos. The issue? They were only five percent of the drivers on the road.[9] Imagine how much racial discrimination in the justice system went uncaptured before video cameras. The justice system blues aren't new, but many people like to act like they are.

Saying black people are natural born criminals also ignores various factors- unemployment, poor schools, corrupt cops, poverty, the ghetto environment- that lead black people into crime. A large chunk of black Americans are raised in ghetto communities designed to ensure widespread mediocrity or failure. Financial disadvantages, unemployment, and lack of neighborhood resources have created a bleak cycle of desperation and crime in many black areas. The government has consciously chosen to avoid making root changes to hood life, instead exploiting its inhabitants for labor and tax revenue.

So again I must ask you if you've ever deeply thought about the meaning of freedom. All of us are free to make choices. Be an omnivore or be a vegan? Be extra and wear thigh high boots to the kickback or chill out in flat sandals? Barber A or Barber B? Netflix or Hulu? The list of choices you have goes on and on, obscuring an ugly reality about freedom behind it. We are not all free, especially when certain choices aren't really available to everyone. The men rounded up and placed in convict leasing programs had no choice in the matter. People say that everyone in prison ended up there made a series of bad choices. Pause. When poor black humans in the present day are tasked with choosing between survival by crime and eviction, hunger, or despair, is it really a choice? When a profitable business has been designed to swallow up as many blacks as possible, is it really the inmates' choices that led them to prison…. or the governments? Is American freedom really freedom if black people are born into a country that sets most of them up for incarceration?

KILLING THE BLACK BODY

What do you see when you walk down the busy streets of the average hood? You pass a packed Popeyes, careen past a chaotic Carls Jr, and march past at least one McDonalds. There is a Wendy's situated between a beauty supply store and a barbershop. A garbage truck roars down the street, minutes from the dump. Depending on the state, there are liquor stores every few blocks, placed neatly next to check cashing places. You'll definitely run into at least two convenience stores. Because most hoods are food deserts, they are more abundant than grocery stores. Convenience store aisles are a menagerie of junk food and sodium packed microwave meals. A few sell bruised bananas, sad salads, and nauseating nachos drenched in neon yellow cheese. Their walls and cracked windows are cramped with ads for every type of cigarette and malt liquor imaginable.

A high volume of these advertisements are for menthol products. I remember Obama's preferred cigarette choice being a punchline quite a few times throughout his presidency. Have you ever given thought to menthol cigarettes as a black stereotype? Have you noticed the truth in it? After all, eighty percent of black smokers reach for menthol cigarettes.[1] During the smoke crazed 1960's, market research showed that black Americans not only enjoyed menthols, but were more likely to believe menthol cigarette related health messaging. "In 1974, before the introduction of lights, Black-menthol smokers, to a greater degree than their White counterparts, believed menthol cigarettes were less hazardous/irritating than other cigarettes."[2] Companies took note and began changing up their advertisements. One popular 1970's era KOOL ad shows a righteous looking black couple with afros and a black power fist clutching a cigarette. Would you be surprised if I told you that the only legal tobacco flavor additive is menthol- despite a few studies that show menthol flavoring makes it harder for smokers to quit? Other flavors like cherry and bubble gum are banned. If that didn't surprise you, try this next one.

Lorillard, the company that sells Newports, distributed free samples of cigarettes to children in urban housing projects in Boston in the 1950s.[3] "Menthol cigarettes have been marketed to some of the most vulnerable segments of the population," research scientist Phillip Gardiner told *The Atlantic*. "For half a century, people with the least resources and the most to lose have been the target of this product."[4] I have always despised the smell of cigarettes, especially Newports. But ever since learning about the nefarious presence of menthol cigarettes in the hood, my hatred of tobacco has increased to formidable levels. My hatred doesn't start and end with the prevalence of menthol or the availability of cigarettes in the hood, however. I am also annoyed with the number of toxic air producing factories and smelly garbage dumps outline our neighborhoods. A study found "a consistent pattern over a 30-year period of placing hazardous waste facilities in neighborhoods where poor people and people of color live."[5] This is especially troubling when

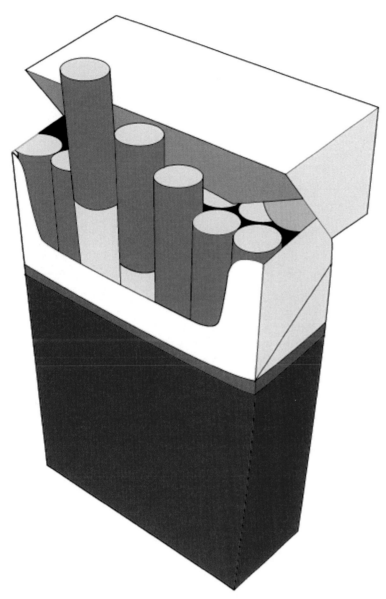

considering that the infant mortality rate among black women is double that of white women.

In addition to the cigarettes and dirty air, food desserts and liquor swamps have got me riled up, too. Food deserts are areas where affordable and nutritious food is sporadic or hard to come by without significant travel. Thirty-six percent of blacks over the age of eighteen are obese—that is roughly ten million of us. Black people eat more fast food than whites and are also forty percent more likely to have high blood pressure.[6] America's worst food deserts are predominately in cities with high numbers of black Americans, including New Orleans, Detroit, and Memphis. With diabetes and heart disease being dire threats to the black community at large, I can only look at the greedy fast food corporations with disgust for placing endless establishments in the hood. They value our dollars and labor, not us. Though food deserts are not exclusively black (and elderly people of all races are a major part of this group), a disproportionate amount of black citizens live in them.

Meanwhile, these same areas are bogged down with liquor stores. One study found that alcohol, especially malt liquor, is more available in poor black neighborhoods than white ones.[7] Upper class and middle class neighborhoods often organize against liquor stores being placed within their boundaries, while disenfranchised and desperate communities don't. Its strange to me that American society scolds and punishes drug dealers but allows tobacco, liquor, and fast food companies to run wild. Maybe its because they run wild in places that don't matter.

The effects of tobacco, fast food, and alcohol on the body are well documented, and yet they remain prevalent in black communities that pump billions of dollars into them every year. I shake with anger when I see a McDonald's commercial pander to black audiences or when I flip past a bizarre Newports advertisement in a black magazine depicting a couple squirting mustard on a chip. These companies profit from our socialized ignorance and apathy of health, effectively killing us for killer profits.

LOOKING FOR DOPE
REPRESENTATION IN TV AND FILM (AND FAILING)

Don't get me wrong. Repugnantly ratchet reality TV like *Love and Hip Hop* is fun to watch. *Scandal* and *Blackish* have dedicated fan bases. Hood classics like *Paid in Full, Belly,* and *Dead Presidents* are enjoyed by many. A lot of people love long dramatic films like *Gone With the Wind, Titanic,* and *Pulp Fiction.* I can name at least five friends who consider *ATL* legendary cinema. Somebody, somewhere, lists *The Help* as one of their favorite movies. Some people will watch anything slave related- *Roots, Underground, 12 Years a Slave, Django, Book of Negroes...* the list goes on and on. Some people even get their sick thrills from Tyler Perry films, basking in the predictable stereotype laced plots that reek of religiosity and respectability politics. But you know what a real geek like me yearns for? More black people in science fiction, historical fiction, and fantasy. Could you imagine a black *Game of Thrones* or a series like *The Walking Dead* where Georgia isn't mostly white people and more than two black guys can exist at one time? Or what about a high budget film fictionalizing iconic pre-colonial African history? I can, but Hollywood can't.

While the easily impressed will lament about the abundance of black faces in film and TV as of late, I can't bite my tongue. A few years of *Scandal* and the prominence of *Empire* doesn't make up for the erasure of the black experience by Hollywood over the past half century. In film particularly, black people have often been presented as flatly one dimensional criminals and subservient beings. The few Oscars won by black people have predominantly been for roles involving maids, criminals, butlers, and slaves. Out of seventeen total Oscars awarded to black people for acting performances over 88 years, nine were for the aforementioned identities. But it's not just about the Oscars. The film industry has mostly been filled with white writers, producers, and directors who have little desire to make movies outside of the norm. The money offered for generic blockbusters has been too green and too available. If they aren't whipping up films about slaves or the civil rights movement (because they love narratives involving black pain), they're producing films to recapture the box office magic of *The Green Mile, Shawshank Redemption, Ghost,* and *The Legend of Bagger Vance.* You know, movies that love to exploit the magical negro trope where black people exist solely to happily help the white main character get over trials and tribulations before neatly disappear-

ing. If studios want laughs, they'll go with Madea or excruciating films like *Soul Plane* or *Get Hard*. The movies filled with reliable buffoonish stereotypes that lack any genuine quality. Coincidently, the movies with these kinds of black characters are the ones with the biggest investment money. This also goes for films with typical historical settings. Despite the abundance of black history to choose from, certain subjects like slavery are constantly rehashed with hefty budgets that little known black history moments can only dream of. When you consider the segregated and homogeneous white communities who get their interactions with black people from VH1 reality shows, negative news representations, gangster rap, athletic events, and predictable Civil Rights movies mandatorily screened during Black History Month, it's no wonder shallow or hateful narratives about black people persist. While there are plenty of shallow depictions of white people on TV, there is an equal balance of reality and depth that keeps them from being dehumanized. Meanwhile black people have much fewer positive depictions to counterbalance all the shallow stereotype laced ones constantly being churned out. There is less authenticity in black films and TV. This is not about respectability politics. I already admitted that I enjoy ratchet TV. This is about offering more dimensions of the black experience that don't leave us susceptible to dehumanization. I am tired of seeing TV and film depictions of black people based on how white people view us. I am tired of black writers pandering to the production dollars, too. But I know it's not their fault. Getting Hollywood to support more black writers, directors, and actors has been a slow march, even though that is where the authenticity comes from.

Diverse black stories from the black point of view deserve to be told in the mainstream. They won't all be awarded like *Moonlight*, but they still deserve to be told. I want to see experiences stretching across income, sex, gender, religion, political, and genre lines without flat dimensional characters that reinforce stereotypes or the status quo. Not all black people relate to the hood films often called classics by those in our community. I don't care for films like *Paid in Full, Dead Presidents,* and *Belly*. I don't laugh at Madea films, *Friday* isn't that funny, and I yawned my way through *The Best Man*. I'm not the only black person who doesn't relate to these films. They are excellent movies to some people, but I just don't relate because I prefer fantasies, apocalyptic dramas, and thrillers. Unfortunately, those films tend to have casts that barely represent people of my color. I'm stuck in the same position with reality TV. *Love and Hip Hop* and *Basketball Wives* aren't black reality. Its generic entertainment that normalizes unhealthy relationships. There should be more shows that showcase black people as interesting AND non-drama oriented. Well, maybe a little bit of drama is ok. But not the kind where the sole premise of the show is pitting black men against women and promoting unhealthy romantic and platonic relationships.

We must demand better representation and make funding the arts a priority. We must support black creatives with our dollars. I am hopeful because the box office success of films like *Get Out* and *Moonlight* prove that black Americans want more than Madea movies, slave cinema, and action heavy films filled with guns and narratives about chasing money. *Get Out* and *Moonlight* weren't typical narratives about the black experience. The accolades they received hint that my future kids will have a larger range of "classics" to choose from than I do. Maybe one day they'll get to binge watch the black *Game of Thrones* that I'm crossing my fingers for.

ASSACARING BLACK LEADERS AND MOVEMENTS

America's traditional response to black people demanding justice and equality is doused in violence, sabotage, and truth distortion. If someone shows too much promise in addressing or dismantling oppression, they are a threat. Just look back through history. The Black Panther Party for Self Defense offered nutrition classes, free breakfast programs, free pest control, free transportation, armed neighborhood patrols, and a number of other services. These programs were too positive and helpful, making the government look bad by comparison. No matter what anyone tries to tell you about Black Panther violence, remember something. Like any other social or political group to ever exist, the Black Panther Party was not without flaws or internal struggles.

But the group wasn't targeted for it's flaws. It was targeted because the Panthers sparked too much confidence in black people and created outspoken critics. The Panthers' flaws were magnified and exploited, not magnified and corrected. On the flip side, their many benefits and contributions were ignored or destroyed.

The purpose of COINTELPRO was to discredit and neutralize opponents and critics of the American government. As such, J Edgar Hoover directed the FBI to collect intel on the Black Panther Party and other extremists utilizing the Ghetto Informant Program in 1967. Barbershop owners and liquor store lookouts granted the FBI access to circles never breached before. Dozens of informants were assigned to the Black Panthers, and they were tasked with spreading misinformation to stir up tension and rivalries. More than anything, Hoover targeted the Black Panther Program to "eradicate its serve the people programs."[1] The same year the Ghetto Informant Program was implemented, a file was started on a gifted and passionate Black Panther named Fred Hampton. He was popular around Chicago, especially after arranging a pact between Chicago's gangs to stop beef and violence. While using an informant named William O'Neil, the FBI sent a series of letters between the Black Panther Party and a Chicago gang known as the Rangers. This created drama, and O'Neil was then tasked with instigating an armed fight between the two in 1969. This destroyed the relationship between the two groups and effectively brought the **43**

pact to an end.

In November 1969, Fred Hampton was in California when two Chicago police officers were killed by Black Panthers after a gunfight. The FBI, hungry to crush Hampton's growing influence, set up a raid for him with local law enforcement and enlisted O'Neal to drug his drink with a pulverized sleeping pill on the same night. On December 3rd, police fired a total of 99 total gunshots after busting through the door of the Panthers' residence. They murdered Mark Clark, who was on security duty. Fred Hampton was shot twice in the head next to his eight-month pregnant fiancé. When recounting the story to the press the next day, police didn't mention any of this. They instead claimed the "extremely vicious" Panthers had attacked them. This worsened the already bad reputation of the Panthers, whose positive community programs were overshadowed by negative reputations in the news.

The FBI, CIA, US Law Enforcement, and American media not only massacred the Black Panther Movement, but discredited and murdered its leaders. Some heavily flawed leaders like Eldridge Cleaver, who encouraged nonsensical actions that hurt the entire movement, didn't need to be murdered or discredited. But many prominent and positive members were targets of extermination. As a result, the Panther's ideology of self sufficiency was murdered. The sense of unity the Panthers fostered among black folks was murdered. Their demand of full rights and their organizing for self sufficiency were crimes to white people, things to be guiltlessly tempered with violence and lies. Tactics also included blackmail and threats. But this wasn't limited to the Panthers. In addition to wiretapping his phones, the FBI sent a letter to Martin Luther King Jr. calling him evil and telling him to kill himself. They even found out about his extramarital affairs and went to the press (though the story never made headway). The FBI also monitored and targeted the Student Non Violent Coordinating Committee (SNCC), the Congress of Racial

Equality (CORE), the National Association for the Advancement of Colored People (NAACP), and the Southern Christian Leadership Conference (SCLC). All of these groups were involved with extinguishing voter discrimination, inequality, and violence against black people. Clearly the government was intent on destroying black progression.

If anything is to be learned from the murdering and discrediting of black leaders and movements, it is that we can not place full responsibility or the burden of knowledge into one or a few leaders. Individual leaders are too susceptible to petty beefs, assassination attempts, and scandals. Not only does too few leaders mean some issues get skimmed over (and others ignored completely), but it means fewer people are in the loop. If everyone is well-versed in the concept of oppression (hence my goal with this book), the murder of a leader or the destruction of a group doesn't stop the momentum. When the Black Panthers weakened after brutal pressure from the government through the 70s and eventually disbanded in 1982, the momentum they had built ended, too. There was less talk of black unity and self reliance and fewer afros, too. We cannot afford to let that happen again. Today's black people have reawakened more ferociously than their 20th century counterparts, and we are only gaining momentum as a collective. Unlike the Panthers and civil rights movement with their few concentrated leaders, today we are much more scattered. In addition to having the internet at our disposal, we are more inclusive and less formal, which gives us an edge over anyone who doesn't want to see us succeed. Confidence and enthusiasm in what we're fighting for (the dismantling of white supremacy) doesn't die with a scandal or a death because our loyalty is to the ideology, not to a particular person.

But that isn't to say our popping black leaders should be tossed aside or that we should let them go without honor. A few of the idolized heroes in our whitewashed grade school textbooks were murderers, rapists, or racists and they still get mentioned for their worthwhile ideas or contributions. See how whiteness works? Too many black names go unmentioned in American textbooks. Or if they are mentioned, they're sanitized and propagandized. Names like Fred Hampton, Assata Shakur, and Malcolm X. Names like Bobby Seale, Huey Newton, and Angela Davis. They should be paid lip service. Their stories are valuable lessons on how to navigate against the oppressors. At the very least, COINTELPRO should be addressed in schools to give students an idea of how the government actively attempted to destroy black progression- less than sixty years ago. People are still alive from that era.

When black people fight back against inequality or organize in large numbers to attack an issue, white victimhood turns us into beastly monsters that need to be dealt with by any means necessary. You know those "race riots" of the late 1800s and the first half of the 20th century? The majority of them were actually factions of white people determined to beat and murder people of color, usually blacks. To call them race riots instead of white acts of terror (or similar) is a repugnant reminder of this country's determination to allow white people to claim victimhood in all racial disputes. When white people are victims, they are allowed to behave in any manner to protect themselves. They then sniff out divisions among our people to create doubt, tension, and confidence, yielding murder and the destruction of black progression.

45

NEGATIVE REPS IN THE NEWS

Back during my junior year of high school when my dream was to be a journalist and meteorologist, I interned at a local TV station, Fox News Charlotte. This was 2011, before Black Lives Matter was conceived. My biggest duty was to pitch news stories and collect tips for the evening news. As a local station it wasn't anything like the nationally syndicated Fox News. It had a younger demographic than other local stations so crimes, community events, local celebrities, and new legislation were the only things that got airtime, not conservative conversations. The evening show was only an hour, so airtime was tight. This meant the producer only went with a quarter of the content suggested from reporters and interns.

For two months, two to three times a week after school I made beat calls to local precincts, checked the tip line, and surreptitiously checked the sites of other news stations for intel. The crime stories I collected were committed by people of all colors, and I'd slide a detailed list of pitches across the evening news producer's desk upon completion. Every week I'd gas myself because at least one of my pitches would make it to air. I barely registered that most of the crime pitches chosen to be articulated on TV involved black criminals. I was just happy to be working at Fox Charlotte, who had more attractive hosts and production sets than the other news outlets.

I cringe in the present knowing that the evening producer who compiled these segments was a black guy.

Looking back, I received tips about crimes and community events, but I didn't receive a single tip about cops doing their jobs correctly. You know those heartwarming photos or stories of white cops peacefully interacting with black Americans? Who sees these moments taking place and decides that it's newsworthy? Aren't the actions documented supposed to be standard cop behavior? If someone were to call the Fox News Charlotte tip hotline when I interned there talking about "a white cop just helped this black kid!", they would have been laughed off of the phone. But in 2017? These kinds of stories just became common after the lightning rod murders of Trayvon Martin, Tamir Rice, and Mike Brown. Remember that widely circulated photo of the black kid hugging the white cop during the aftermath of Ferguson civil unrest? Blue Lives Matter advocates everywhere ignored the actual problem of police brutality in favor of the staged hug, using it as a reason to lambast protestors as irrational thugs. Promoting these kinds of news stories belittle police brutality and other black issues, but the dark role of media outlets in our oppression goes much deeper.

White people and their news outlets have been slandering black people since at least the 18th century. They have had the social and economic power to build reputable media houses, in which inferior citizens were rarely empathized with. To sell papers, many newspapers also engaged in sensationalism, meaning at any time a 5-foot-7 black man could become an 8-foot giant negro with supernatural strength. It is a familiar narrative built on the back of popular negro stereotypes. Black people are savage, angry, and violent, whereas white people are civilized and good.

After a slew of slave rebellions and conspiracies that were not considered justified by white society, a 19th century newspaper cartoon warned of sneaky slaves desiring to switch places with massa, effectively sowing mistrust among slaveholders and even their most beloved of property. During post reconstruction and the nadir of American race relations, the black-on-white rape myth was pedaled by newspapers across the country. Thanks to a 1914 New York Times article, Americans became fearful of cocaine crazed black people who were unfazed by bullets and hungry for violence.[1] All the while, white newspapers were peppered with sympathetic or forgiving stories about lynch mobs slaughtering black men.

Bias has always negatively skewed black news stories to impact sympathy for black issues. Coverage of the Watts Riots of 1965, like the riots after the Rodney King verdict twenty-six years later, were devoid of context about police brutality and local discrimination against black citizens. They were simply thugs destroying their own neighborhood. Even trying to do things peacefully was twisted by the news. In 1967 when the armed Black Panthers of Oakland peacefully interrupted a city hall meeting, they were lampooned by the news as violent thugs- in a state where openly carrying loaded weapons was legal. This is just one example of negative news bias.

From 1967 to 1992, blacks accounted for 57% of the severely impoverished people depicted in popular magazines, twice the true proportion of poor blacks.[2] Their poverty was not only magnified, but blamed on laziness, drug problems, broken families, and addiction to welfare instead of being explained by harmful systemic policies. In the 1980s, there were dramatic exposés of black welfare queens and cracked out single mothers intercut with footage from dingy crack dens and trap houses being raided by the Drug Enforcement Agency. In the 1990s emerged the concept of the super predator, who social scientists alleged was a type of remorseless teenager growing in population. The super predator was heavily associated with black teenagers, many of whom were reeling from the effects of the 80's crack era.

When news outlets reported on the erroneous phenomenon, most footage involved black teens. "We're talking about kids who have no respect for human life and no sense of future… they kill or maim on impulse without any intelligible motive." said John Dilulio in 1995.[3] The narrative didn't stop at the teenagers, either. News outlets ran daily stories on the crimes of black people at disproportionate levels when compared to their white peers. In the 21st century, this practice is still common. Now that instances of cop brutality are available on film and people can see that murder-by-cop isn't always justified, the black criminal stereotype is necessary for white Americans to keep giving bad police officers free passes. Think of how unjustly slain black women, men, and children are memorialized by media outlets using mug shots. When there are no mug shots, there are other tactics used to present a negative view of the murder victim. For instance, when Tamir Rice was killed one vile media outlet published an entire story on the criminal history of Tamir's parents.

The willingness to leave context out of events of black civil unrest and to disproportionately showcase black on white crime in the news has certainly impacted race relations. News outlets routinely dehumanize black Americans to justify discrimination against them. Representation matters, especially for people who rarely encounter black folk outside of media and pop culture. Consider the 2014 study that showed 75% of white people don't have black friends because they're more likely to live and work in self-segregated homogenous populations.[4] Predominantly negative and skewed news narratives guide white people's views on legislation, race relations, and police brutality scenarios. The news also encourages how white people interact with black people in real life. News outlets know this, but they stick to their lanes of profitable comfort and stereotypes. They use mug shots for unarmed blacks slain by cops and speculate on whether or not Black Lives Matter is as dangerous as a group that wore white hoods, lynched thousands, and terrified millions. Those same outlets will still post cheerful images of white mass shooters and murderers, they'll keep producing glossy interview specials with Nazis, and they'll even continue to sensationalize pictures of white cops doing their jobs correctly… while also claiming that there's no room in journalism for favoritism or bias.

OBVIOUSLY RACIST STUFF

Dragging yourself out of bed for an 8 AM class several times a week is one of the most torturous things about college. You often lay in your bed as your alarm blares, wondering if you really need to go, desperately trying to remember the attendance policy as you flutter in and out of sleep. Every time you muster the energy to take an appallingly short shower (if you have time to take one at all) and slide on some pants to scramble out of the dorm, you desperately hope the next hour rolls by so that you can scamper back to your twin bed, fiending for more sleep like an addict. You do not, however, hope to hear a white classmate say during a class discussion that "racism is over because the KKK isn't around anymore, black people aren't slaves, and they have BET and Obama." That was my freshman year at The Ohio State University, before I truly understood the magnitude of systematic oppression, but I remember it like it was yesterday. The topic at hand wasn't even racism, but American reality TV shows and morality. At the time I didn't believe racism was a serious problem but my southern childhood had ensured I knew it wasn't dead either. Her conviction about the matter was annoying, but I didn't say anything because I didn't want to be the angry black girl. A few classmates nodded their heads in slight concurrence as my professor's stoic face turned to the next commentator. Over the next few years, I'd hear similar opinions from a fare share of white college classmates.

While I continued to learn more about racism as an entire system and not just the actions of white people, many of my classmates must have not been paying attention. When they thought of racism, they envisioned slavery, the KKK, lynching, and black people being dragged through the streets and beaten during the civil rights movement. The attitudes of my former Ohio State classmates mirrored a number of angry white people who verbally attack me on Twitter, but with way fewer expletives. Why? I blame overt racism and its prominent representation in American schools. Our public school curriculum teaches racism in a neat way so as not to offend anyone or make white students feel guilty, in addition to reinforcing the status quo.

The scope of black oppression in school textbooks is limited. Basic high school history **49**

curriculum hustles right past the discriminatory War on Drugs initiated in the 1980s and the sly re-segregation of American schools. The KKK is one of hundreds of militant white supremacist groups that exist now, and on internet forums they're considered one of the tamer hate groups… but you don't hear about any of that. The widespread shooting of unarmed black teenagers, kids, and adults is the new lynching, but it is not discussed that way in textbooks. Furthermore, schools don't explain that slavery has been replaced by the private prison industry or that dragging black people through the streets still happens during lawfully assembled protests and marches. Black people are still paid less money than their peers in professional fields. My high school history teachers never told me that voters are still nefariously disenfranchised in many states, through discriminatory voting restrictions that don't dare mention race to appear neutral. None of this is mentioned in American public school textbooks.

Instead, students get a tidy wrap up of the civil rights movement that doesn't go past the 1970s if their teachers don't feel like exploring racism further. Students graduate from high school convinced that because obviously racist stuff is rightfully condemned, racism is over. They believe our country is truly equal for everyone. They haven't been taught to see racism as an entire oppressive system, but instead as the actions of a few people. Because most white people today don't embody overtly racist values, they feel good about themselves and the state of race relations, declining to analyze further. They don't understand the concepts of white privilege, micro aggressions, or coded language so they unwittingly dabble in all three. They complain about victims of police brutality as 'thugs" without considering circumstances or historical parallels. They don't think black natural hair is professional, because they subconsciously process white natural hair as the standard. They claim to not see color, erasing blackness and the corresponding realities for their comfort. They even say conversations about racism are divisive, choosing to ignore actual problems at their benefit. Even worse, many of these same kinds of white people see justice, reparations, or attention given to black people and issues as unfair to them and infringing on their rights. They don't understand what leveling the playing fields means because most American schools convincingly perpetuate the notion that we live in a harmonious and equal post racial society. A meritocratic America with justice and equal opportunity for all.

But we don't live in that America. It's a society of uncanny delusion where the response to "Black Lives Matter" is "WHITE LIVES MATTER TOO!" Black people are also drinking that strange Kool-Aid. This is a society where black celebs drunk on money, power, and fame claim that people who aren't as successful as them only complain about racism because they're lazy. A place where crystal clear videos of police brutality are considered to be not enough evidence for murder convictions or even terminated employment. This is the land of employee grooming restrictions; ones that target Jamal and his dreadlocks but keep Hannah and her messy buns safe from harm. It is a place where entire historical records of racism, deceit, and cruel systemic design are omitted from public conversations about modern day Chicago and Baltimore. A place that employs a sanitized curriculum involving a comfortable narrative of racism and neo-conservatism for the benefit of white people. You know. The kind of place where a white student will make your 8 AM American Pop Culture class more miserable than it already is; because of their pathetic belief that overt racism is the only kind of racism there is.

POLICE BRUTALITY

In 2016 and early 2017, a number of outlets began breaking news that has been common knowledge in the black community for a long time: white supremacists are infiltrating law enforcement. Even when the FBI delivered the news in 2006 to deaf ears, they still weren't ahead of the black curve. Black people have been experiencing discrimination, ego, and sadism at the hands of white law enforcement members for centuries now. Slave patrols began in 1704, which intensified in 1831 after Nat Turner's rebellion. They made white citizens feel safe from insurrection, so there was little public interest in regulating their abusive behavior towards slaves and free black people. When post-emancipation police forces assembled, their job was quite similar to slave patrols: keep black people in line and keep white people safe. Many of these newly christened police officers were confederate veterans and former slave owners with grudges. In 1866 an altercation between white police officers (many of whom were former confederate soldiers) and black union soldiers led to white mobs of civilians and police murdering, robbing, and raping dozens of blacks before setting fire to roughly 100 homes, church-  es, and schools. The terror didn't stop there. For years to come, police harassed, beat, and killed innumerable amounts of black citizens with little interference from the public because their job was to protect the public. Cruel cop behavior became exponentially more valid each time brutality was tolerated or excused. Sometimes cop cruelty meant doing nothing while a white mob attacked a black person. Other times it was donning a KKK hood and stringing a negro up from a tree after a long shift as the county sheriff. Over a century without widespread proper punishment for discrimination has made police untouchable to criticism. White and deluded minorities alike scream "Blue Lives Matter" without consideration of the original purpose of police.

No matter the crime (or lack of one), anyone labelled as criminal has traditionally been allowed to be—even expected to be— treated as inferiors. This is of course unless the color of their skin or weight of their wallet makes them appear more innocent. But blackness has widely been associated with crime, since those days of slave rebellions when desiring freedom was a punishable offense. American society has become desensitized to the treatment of criminals largely in part because people choose to ignore what drives a person into crime in the first place. Since slavery was abolished, America has crafted narratives for black people that justify violence against them at the hands of police and civilians alike. At the root of the narratives is the scary black trope, the dangerous criminal who needs to be handled by any means necessary. The orig- **51** inal criminals were slaves and runaways, guilty only of being black and wanting more out of life. Then there is the still surviving fear of freed black men looking for retribution between white women's thighs. The sexually deviant criminal narrative wasn't limited to black men, either. During the first half of the 20th century, black women were frequently arrested and prosecuted for solicitation, at rates higher than that of their white peers. In the second half of the twentieth century, it was the so-called black extremists who were criminals and terrorists. Then came the gangbangers, drug dealers, and crack mothers who needed to be squared away out of sight from white society. In none of these scenarios were we thought of as people, or legitimate citizens. Therefore, there is no consideration for circumstance, no outrage at how we are treated.

Over time, the white public and economically privileged have swallowed false news narratives, disproportionate crime reports, and propaganda that minimalizes the effects of police brutality. They ignore hardened reports and genuine experiences because police can't be checked. "They keep us safe!" they say, as if that means acts of discrimination and brutal force shouldn't be punished—or even commented on. In January 2017 when the Department of Justice released a scathing report citing clear police brutality in Chicago, Blue Lives and All Lives Matter constituents stayed silent, proving yet again that their message was really all about white lives. Police clearly know they can fudge their reputations for the general public, too. The government doesn't even keep an official record of how many people are killed in cop encounters! Since 2011, less than 3% of the nation's 18,000 state and local police agencies have reported fatal shootings to the FBI.[1] I'm reminded of the sad fact that the government did not record the number of lynch murders that occurred throughout the 19th and 20th centuries. Social media and camera phone footage has made revelations about police brutality come to light but these things have always been noted in the black community. The injustice is still painful. Even with more visibility, many victims of police brutality still receive no justice. For example, of the twenty reported unarmed police murders from 2014 to 2015, zero involved shooters were convicted of murder.[2]

Police do have important jobs. If I get robbed, you better believe I'll be calling them. If I'm ever lost in Brooklyn on my way to the Bronx with a dead phone battery at 3 in the morning as I have been before, I definitely will approach a cop for directions. But if I see a video of a cop rolling up to a 12-year-old black boy and hopping out of the car to shoot him before even asking his name, I'm going to ask questions. If I hear about a black man holding a bee bee gun in a store selling bee bee guns and then being shot in cold blood, I am going to criticize and ask that the cop be held accountable. Same goes for a man selling loose cigarettes. If he gets put in an illegal chokehold and dies, I've got some damned thoughts on the matter. Unfortunately, not everyone shares my mentality. On one side, many of my own people do not feel comfortable and safe around people who are supposed to protect and serve them... under any circumstances. On the other side lies those with unyielding support for police... also under any circumstances. The support is partly borne from intensely misinformed nationalism, but at the core many white Americans are reluctant to discuss or reprimand police brutality due to their innate hatred for those they see as inferior. Their approval or dismissal of how cops treat black criminals is rooted in society's dehumanization of them.

QUADROONS, #TEAMLIGHTSKINNED, & OTHER TENTACLES OF COLORISM

One of my ugliest memories from the early days of twitter are the #TeamLightSkinned and

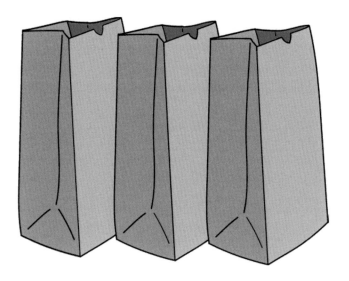

#TeamDarkSkinned hashtags. 2009 twitter was the Wild West. It was already a cesspool of insensitivity and ignorance (and fun), but these hashtags were especially nasty. They were not only inserted into bios but sprinkled onto the timeline to initiate debates over the merits of redbones over yellow bones and whether or not dark-skinned women should wear red lipstick. Being the uninformed teenager that I was, I engaged in the trend just like I had since childhood, when I heard from a disapproving and revered family member that I looked too dark from playing outside. From that moment, I associated dark skin with inferiority. I didn't go around calling dark-skinned girls cock-roaches like some of my more brutal peers, but

I was still a garbage individual. Back in those days I repeated the jagged phrase "Light skinned girls never go out of style," insinuating that brown and dark-skinned girls did. I remember a 5th grade classmate whispering to me that I was prettier than the few other black girls in our class, because I had the "prettiest skin". I believed her and cherished her compliment. Later in middle school I was plump and rife with insecurities. When boys or rap songs opined about their love for light skinned girls, my insecure ass latched onto the concept that my skin color was somehow superior to my dark skinned counterparts. If I got into it with a dark-skinned girl, the ensuing argument or fight involved taunts about her skin color. I look back on this time with shame, shuddering about my once prized role as a light-skinned person in a community that actively promotes colorism. And yet during the whole time that I looked down my nose at darker wom-en, whenever I envisioned myself as an adult I saw a confident dark-skinned woman in a red lingerie set eating strawberries in bed.

It was not uncommon for light-skinned slaves to consider themselves better than their darker counterparts. The mixed race and fair-skinned children of slave owners often found themselves on the receiving end of special treatment and privileges. Because whiteness was idealized and darkness demonized, light-skinned female slaves fetched higher prices at auction. Quadroons possessed 1/4 black ancestry, mulattos had 1/2 black ancestry, and both were considered more beautiful and therefore more valuable than their darker sisters. There was a sizeable amount of mixed race slaves that gained freedom but most toiled away in bondage, albeit often with jobs in the big house or with slackened constraints. They got special privileges and had better chances at learning how to read. White people had long before instilled the idea that dark skin was inferi-or and dirty, a sentiment echoed since the 18th century in art and soap advertisements. Lighter skinned black people mirrored their superiority complexes.

After slavery, white society continued its favor of lighter skinned black Americans. While **53** dark-skinned women continued to be portrayed as unattractive, asexual, and sloppy in main-stream media well into the 20th century, light-skinned women were considered more attractive and desirable by comparison. But it wasn't just white America that had something against dark people. The small middle class black community pushed colorism onto their own. Several esteemed black churches and social clubs required prospective members to be lighter than paper bags. Popular HBCUs asked for photos from applicants to weed out dark skinned people. Even Howard University showed preferential treatment to light-skinned applicants and students. There was a distinct hierarchy for black people based on skin color that also plagued the lower class. Lighter skinned blacks were both envied and placed on pedestals if they weren't accused of being inauthentic. To add to the colorism drama, super light skinned blacks were encouraged to move away from their families and pass as white. They often did this to varying degrees of success. One example is Dr. Albert Johnston, who passed as white for twenty years to practice medicine with his extremely pale and blue-eyed black wife. The couple even had children who were passed off as white. The 1949 movie "Loose Boundaries" was a dramatized version of their lives.

Colorism reeks of a mixture of self-hatred brought on by white supremacy and America's willingness to tolerate lighter skinned black people more than darker ones. For some, latching onto the privileges that light skin granted was an instinctive form of survival. In turn, dark skins often questioned light skinned people's authenticity.

Back to me and my fantasies of being dark skinned. While I believed myself to not be black enough, I saw dark skinned black people as too black. It wasn't until I was 18 that I realized I was a hater. It was something I had learned from family and environment. I envied dark skinned black girls and their beautiful skin as I did my part to temper their collective self-esteem. I was a colorist. While loads of light skinned black people have become aware of the privilege they wield, lighter skin has not stopped being idealized. Colorism has permeated society. The result of so many years of brainwashing has created squadrons of black people on social media and in real life who defend their insults of dark-skinned women as just being about preference. You know, the type of people who say "You're pretty for a dark skinned girl." It's not just men, either. Many light-skinned women, like I once did, join in on the marginalization of their darker sisters. It doesn't help that prominent celebrities are often lightened in their photos or have actually been lightened in real life. Light skin continues to be lusted after. There are jars of skin lightener available at your nearest beauty supply store. Dark-skinned female leads not playing mammies and maids has only just become more common, but they still don't get the screen time they deserve. Furthermore, darker black women are still overwhelmingly underrepresented in rap videos and lyrics. The simple person will ask why this matters, dismissing the unheard desires of their darker nieces, daughters, sisters, cousins, and aunts who would love to have more dark skinned women represented and adored in mainstream media. But colorism isn't just a problem for black women, nor is it just about representation. Colorism has dangerous and disadvantageous effects on black people. It affects relationships, employment, and treatment in the justice system. For example, one study showed that among 66,927 male felons incarcerated for their first offense in Georgia from 1995-2002, the darker skinned men received the longest prison sentences compared to their light and white peers.[1] My skin color shouldn't give me social and employment advantages that my darker skinned peers don't have. Colorism is a leftover from slavery, rewarmed and re-served as the years have gone by. I don't want any of it on my plate.

RESPECTABILITY POLITICS

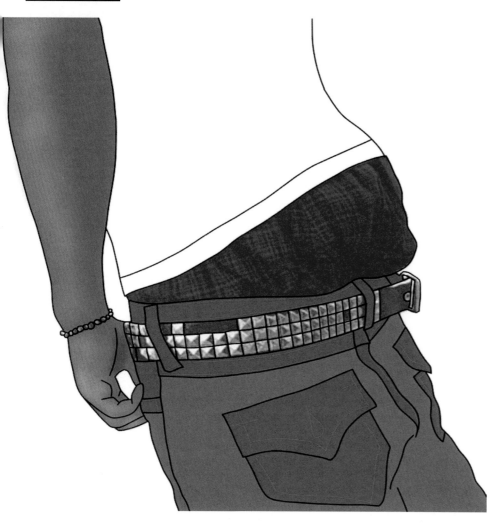

Maybe it's my age and hood origin, but I'm indifferent to baggy pants. The sight of a black man in pants below his waist does nothing to arouse my interest, let alone stir any type of rage. But if you ask the average black person over 30? The topic of baggy pants sets their tongues ablaze with fury and disgust. "This is why they don't respect us now!" he or she spits out angrily. Right… because our ancestors were enslaved and hung from trees because of their outfit choices. It is respectability politics, not baggy pants, that disgust me.

"Are you not paying attention, people with their hat on backwards, pants down around the crack?" screeched Bill Cosby during his infamous 2004 Pound Cake speech. Of all the shucking and jiving the now disgraced Cosby did in that oratorical atrocity, a particular line stands out. "The white man, he's laughing, got to be laughing. Fifty percent drop out, rest of them in prison." I'll chalk up the exaggerated statistic to artistic license, but Cosby himself was being very honest when he shelled out this line. But not in the way the average Uncle Tom thinks. For centuries black people have been trying to wriggle out of the vicious violence and discrimination inflicted upon us because of our skin color. At every turn there has been a privileged group of negroes preaching that any racism black people experience comes from their blatant lack of self respect. This shtick relies on finding a type of black person to blame for why white people are racist. It also involves alleviating blame from white people and ignoring systems of oppression. One of the earliest examples of preaching respectability politics came from Booker T Washington. In an 1895 speech delivered against the receding haze of reconstruction, Washing-

55

ton declared that black people "should not permit our grievances to overshadow our opportunities." He rebuked black Americans for seeking political power instead of "real estate or industrial skill." As white America did not want black people in politics, Washington thought the respectable thing would be to stay out of politics. His goal was to maintain white comfort. He thought that backing off white territory would make whites play nice. That is respectability politics- doing things in a way that doesn't make the dominant group feel offended, guilty, or troubled in the hope that it will keep you safe from harm. Clearly, Washington underestimated how cruel and discriminatory all-white Jim Crow era governments would be.

Respectability politics most often encompass denouncing things that are associated with black people, even if white people partake in those same things. Baggy pants, loud rap music, Ebonics, and hoodies are some of the most common examples that come to mind. Respectability politics are naïve because they operate on the assumption that assimilation will protect black people from harm. After the widespread sexual abuse of black women during and immediately after slavery, black community leaders agonized over a way to strike back against white on black rape. So they decided to concentrate their efforts on cleaning up the black woman's image. The white woman's image was of purity and virtue, while black women were seen as the complete opposite. It became a serious desire of middle class negro women to separate themselves from the loose jezebel reputation attached to all black females. The same went for middle class black men, who were propagandized as hypersexual beasts. Even if white people behaved in a way that could be categorized as loose or hypersexual, the reputation, which justified sexual abuse and violence, was not attached to all of them. So looking respectable— nuclear families, proper clothes, proper hair, proper public decorum— was supposed to be a shield of assimilation for black people against discrimination or ill reputations. The problem? Skin color has always been the true problem, not behavior. So despite efforts by black leaders to fix our reputations through rebranding our images, black women continued being prime targets of sexual assault and black men continued being rapists in the eyes of white society.

When a racist cop unloads his weapon into the back of a fleeing black suspect, he is not pausing to evaluate whether or not the man has on baggy pants, speaks ebonics, or goes to church every Sunday. Similarly, when a rapist penetrates a woman against her will, he does not pause beforehand to ask her what her body count is or how many one night stands she has had. The kicker? If racists or rapists do ask these questions and use the answers to justify brutality, they're still garbage. There are no excuses for brutality. Black human beings universally deserve the same rights as the dominant group of white people, regardless of class, occupation, code switching abilities, or intelligence levels. Using trends, fads, or toxic behavior of black people to justify violence or discrimination against them is oppressive. As a black person, talking at length about "how blacks disrespect themselves" without bringing up systemic oppression is traitorous. Respectability politics denies accountability for racial predators (and sexual ones too). Uttering the phrase "this is why they don't respect us" is a bareback admission of catering to white gaze, superiority, and fragility. You have made maintaining their comfort- instead of securing complete and total equality- the ultimate goal.

STEREOTYPES

I'm awesome at twerking. I can't actually do any other types of dancing because I barely have rhythm. My father is a deadbeat. I hate watermelon and hot sauce. I do love fried chicken. I cry when I watch The Color Purple. I could go the rest of my life without hearing a Michael Jackson song and I'd be just fine. I prefer tequila to Hennessy, but the latter was my college standby. Clearly I both embody black stereotypes and defy them. But there are some others- namely the Jezebel and Angry Black Woman- that I can't escape. There have been many moments in my early life where I remember holding my tongue so that nobody would think I was being irrational or mean. Even in the present day I take special care when ordering my food at restaurants because I'm worried someone will spit in my meal if they develop the slightest notion that I'm an angry black woman.

The world is filled with stereotypes. I get it. Irish people drink a lot. Redheads have terrible tempers. Asians are smart and meek. But in America, where the population is roughly 77% white and 13% black, stereotypes have a harsh effect on black people. I'm not talking about black people liking watermelon or fried chicken, though those are annoying stereotypes too. I'm talking about the debilitating stereotypes that impact justice, influence violence, and increase apathy for black issues. Think about the black thug and criminal stereotypes. Black boys and men face the most risk from these dehumanizing categories that reduce them from people to dangerous threats. The most agonizing part about this trope is its origin in systematic disadvantage.

When people bark "what about black on black crime?!" to shut down police brutality conversations, they are making a few mistakes. First of all, black on black crime is no different from white on white crime. 81% of whites who are murdered are murdered by other whites. Using that statistic alone, should we not try to prevent terrorist attacks because white Americans have no respect for each other? Secondly, they are also insinuating that human beings should be subjected to cruelty because of their status as criminals. Lastly, they are denying that cops should be held to a higher standard than criminals.

Black stereotypes exist to snatch away human status and ultimately victimhood. The sexually insatiable black brute, extremely popular post-emancipation, justified the lynching of thousands of black men at the hands of white men who feared the rape of their women. Though most black men were lynched for daring to vote or owning a business, many were lynched because of the brute stereotype. Meanwhile, black women, who had been relegated to a similar status before slavery, continued being wanton jezebels that no man could technically rape because they always wanted sex. While black men hung from trees, scores of black women were raped and sexually exploited by men of both colors who didn't see them as actual humans.

Another popular black stereotype that gets a lot of traction is that we're all fatherless. After breeding us for centuries and separating fathers from their children the entire time, white society had the gall to blame poor familial relationships on our inferiority later in the 20th century. The prevalence of fatherless families was only worsened by lynching epidemics and the justice system blues. Several states furthered the issue of fatherless black families in the 50s and 60s when they enacted "man in the house" rules that forbade able bodied adult men from living in welfare supported homes. The fatherless stereotype is just a slap in the face.

These stereotypes are rooted in historical malignancy, steeped in racism, and sometimes spiked with sexism or classism. Some are a trifecta of all three, like the Welfare Queen. She made her first appearance in Jet Magazine in 1974 in the form of Linda Taylor. She had dozens of fake names, was racially ambiguous enough to claim various ethnicities, and even switched up her occupations to collect on different insurance and welfare schemes. Dubbed the "Welfare Queen", it didn't take long for the name to latch onto black women around the hood who used welfare to make ends meet. The economy was beginning to fail, and the image of a black woman exploiting the system was not a good look. Even though welfare fraud was largely a male dominated category during the 60s and early 70s and more white people were on welfare at the time, the concept of welfare and related fraud really found a home in black people.

Republican politicians led legions of their poor white constituents to vote against their class interests thanks to the Welfare Queen stereotype. It was particularly easy for Republican politicians to call for the termination or downsizing of welfare programs when black women were the face of them, because black women have traditionally been seen as lesser beings who don't deserve help or comfort. This is borne of hatred for black women, also called misogynoir. The welfare queen narrative also took hold because politicians called people on welfare lazy, a stereotype that has been attached to black people since the post-slavery days when they refused to sign labor contracts.

Another harmful stereotype about black women is the infamously angry and bitter sapphire, also known as the angry black woman. The stereotype was a response to black women shedding their overtly-submissive slavery era masks. It has been a popular mainstay in various forms of popular media since the *Amos n' Andy* radio show in 1943. Legitimate reasons to be angry cast aside, black women can't voice negative opinions or offer critique without being called bitter or irrational…. meaning that whatever we're saying often goes unheard. One area this impacts is our relationships with black men. To avoid hatred or accusations of man-hating, black women often don't voice their opinions on important issues. Because critiquing the toxic behavior of black men is seen as bitterness or anger, very valid opinions often aren't listened to. Embodying the angry black woman stereotype has historically put women in danger of domestic violence, dismissal, or retribution.

There are some positive sounding stereotypes. Or at least ones that sound positive. We can dance, we can sing, we're good at cooking. Notice how these all pertain to entertainment value? Even the super positive sounding "superhuman" trope might make you feel a little proud until you realize it was exacerbated by early 20th century reports of cocaine fueled blacks unstoppable by bullets and impervious to pain. This is a concept that prevails even today, in the minds of doctors and police alike. The stereotype also contributes to the belief that our superior athleticism is a valid reason to doubt our intellectual abilities.

TOMS AND TRAITORS

The man who inspired the titular character of Harriet Beecher Stowe's 1852 novel *Uncle Tom's Cabin* was named Josiah Henson. He spent approximately 40 years as his master's most faithful servant before being swindled by him when attempting to purchase his freedom. On a trip to New Orleans, he found out he was going to be sold. He briefly considered murdering his white overseer and companions, but couldn't bring himself to do it because he was a Christian. He escaped into Canada and started a settlement for former slaves and became an abolitionist, eventually publishing his autobiography. Stowe twisted Josiah into Uncle Tom, a suffering, passive, and deeply religious lifelong slave loyal to his masters. In the end of the novel he is beaten to death for not divulging the whereabouts of three female runaways.

Over time, Uncle Tom became a term that embodied black people too subservient and endeared to the white race. Whether it was beaten into them or learned early from childhood, filling the role of inferior was known to every slave. They didn't talk back or cause trouble because it would have gotten themselves and others in trouble. Some slaves developed a twisted love for the masters who treated them like children and/or complete trash. Though the character Uncle Tom was not an Uncle Tom in the modern sense of complete subservience (because he didn't sell out the three escaped women), slavery was rife with black men and women dedicated to white people. It was also filled with traitors. Perhaps sensing how advantageous it would be to have a divided

black community, it wasn't surprising that many masters cultivated favorite slaves or encouraged competition for his affection (or protection from his wrath). Affection could mean gifts, status, power, or preferential treatment from overseers. Slaves who snitched on others could be rewarded with extra food or some hand-me-down clothing. In exchange, they earned reputations from more rebellious slaves as niggers to distrust or avoid completely. These slavery era traitors were definitely manipulated or abused into white devotion, but didn't cease to exist after emancipation. Post-slavery Toms and traitors were motivated by the same factors as their pre-antebellum counterparts- gifts, power, status, protection- and also lacked in racial pride or a connection to their own people. They were complicit in harming the black community for their own gain. For example, take black Chicago city alderman Claude Holman. In 1958, a white liberal alderman sponsored a city ordinance that forbade property owners and real estate agents from racially discriminating against buyers. Claude, who was one of Mayor Daly's faithful servants, attacked the ordinance and stalled its progression by adding stipulations to make it virtually ineffective by the time it was passed five years later.[1]

Like the Uncle Toms and traitors who have existed throughout American history, I am both disgusted and sorry for the Ben Carsons and Omarossas of the world. Self-hatred and white supremacy has combined to create a brand of blackness hell-bent on being the most prized kind of black. The black that white people can trust, love, and feel comfortable around. They don't feel like they have value if white people don't accept them. Therefore, they don't challenge white racism. Instead they allow it to exist unchecked or they perpetuate it themselves. They dutifully spread misinformation in an attempt to divide our ranks further. It isn't always clear to some members of the community when a prominent black person is shucking and jiving for white people, usually because of a lack of knowledge in certain areas. I was stunned when I heard a Trump-hating family member (who I'm quite fond of) defend Steve Harvey for meeting with the newly elected president. She and millions of others who enjoy Family Feud couldn't see the traitorous opportunity thinly veiled as a diplomacy mission. My family member, who knows nothing about why Chicago is so violent, supported Steve's assertion that he was meeting with Donald Trump to strategize change in Chicago. If Steve Harvey had ever before addressed the systematic racism that caused violence and despair in Chicago, perhaps I'd be more inclined to believe that he met with Trump to discuss strategies. But my gut (and mostly everybody else's), tells me that the meeting was for Harvey to boost his own visibility and gain favor with the Trump administration.

Toms and traitors are dangerous for another reason. They are the black people to whom white racists and racism deniers point to when trying to prove their points. Toms and traitors legitimize bad arguments from white people and drown out any dissenting thoughts. Some people will claim "but white people sell out their own people too," which is correct… but it isn't a valid excuse for black traitors. Because white people have the majority of the social, political, and economic power in this country, they can afford to sell each other out. Black people cannot. Allowing Toms and traitors to flourish with our support is a mistake we cannot afford to keep making.

UNCHECKED MENTAL HEALTH

Black Americans are the least likely group to commit suicide.[1] Before celebrating, ingest a study by Mental Health America that revealed 56% of black Americans believe depression to be a normal part of aging.[2] Despite being crippling, toxic, and debilitating, 56% of our people think that severe dejection and sadness is meant to be suffered through with a quiet dignity. Why? For one thing, mental health care can be costly and roughly 40% of blacks rely on public health insurance, which is often minimal in coverage. But it's more than that. After all, black people have suffered under centuries of abuse and degradation without too much commotion or complaint. While we could have bombed buildings, formed lynch mobs to hang white rapists, or set crosses on fire in our yards to let crackers know we meant business, we largely chose non-violence and patience. We did it out of necessity borne from the days when one wrong sideways glance at massa could earn you a merciless beating. Through all the trauma, black people learned to be

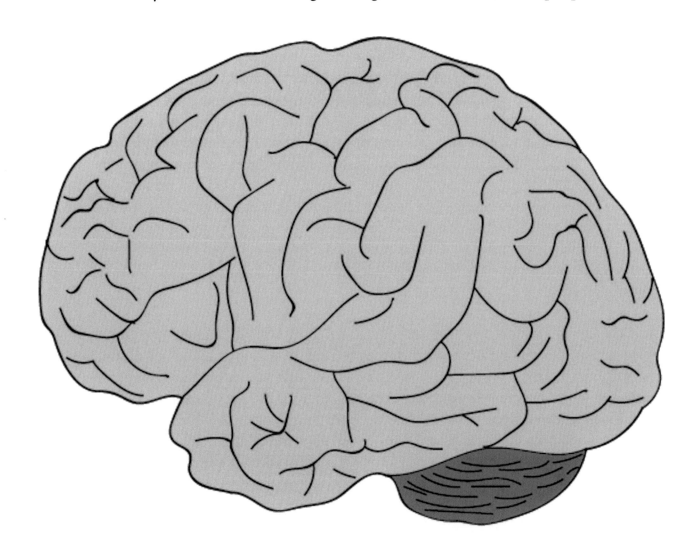

strong in the face of racism, even if their insides (and outsides) were being ripped apart. Perhaps this is why a good chunk of black people believe therapy is "a white thing." Adding to the misery is the fact that 90% of mental health professionals are white.[3] Black folks have traditionally told their problems to God or trusted peers, not to mental health physicians. Their fear and mistrust of these doctors wasn't completely unfounded, either. In the 1970s and 1980s psychiatric scholars were claiming that "African Americans didn't have the mental capacity to become depressed."[4] You can see how this blatantly racist attitude might render a mental health physician useless to a black person suffering from depression. Depressed minds often turn to drugs and alcohol to self medicate. If today's hip-hop lyrics don't make that clear to you, I'm not sure what will.

But depression isn't the only type of mental disorder going unchecked among our people. Because black people of all ages are more likely than their white peers to experience violence, they are more likely to experience post-traumatic stress disorder. Think of all of our ancestors who have been passing along traumatized outlooks and habits to their children over the centuries. They often did not verbally voice their pain… they just let it explode out and seep into their homes and lives. Speaking of emotional explosions, bipolar disorder rates are as common in black Americans as white Americans but we are less likely to seek treatment. To some black people, claiming to have a mental disorder is seen as an excuse. "We got through slavery and Jim Crow without psychiatrists!" declares Hotep Hykeem, ignoring the fact that black people are just as likely as (if not more than) their white peers to suffer from mental disorders. "You need Jesus, that's all!" claims Christian Claudette, ignoring the fact that black women are more likely to experience depression than their white and male peers… and more likely to be self-identified Christians.

Sweeping mental health issues under the rug isn't helpful to the black community and neither is hoping Jesus will wash away people's disorders. The intersection of these two attitudes has created an environment in which many of our people don't feel comfortable checking on the state of their mental health. When you group this with the average black American's financial struggles and white therapists who can be insensitive to racial issues, it's easy to see why mental health goes unchecked. Instead of seeking help, we often bottle up our emotions until we lash out and hurt others. It's a damned shame too, because we can't keep raising generations of children who inherit our problems and repressed trauma. Speaking of the next generation, suicide rates are up among black teenagers. Suicide rates for kids between ages 5 and 11 have doubled.[5] Suicide is the third leading cause of death among blacks aged 15-24. Suicide is especially prevalent among black transgender youth, and transgender blacks of all ages are at higher risk of shaky mental health, suicide attempts, and completed suicides.[6]

Being proactive about good mental health not only increases quality of live and improves relationships, but starts the next generation on a smoother foundation. We need more mental health advocates, more black mental health physicians, and more black mental health safe spaces. Our ancestors weren't allowed to unload their mental burdens, but we can.

VOTER USE AND ABUSE

After Lyndon B. Johnson signed the Civil Rights Act of 1964 (privately known as the nigger bill), he told his press secretary "I think we just delivered the south to the Republican party for a long time to come."[1] After this legislation, black loyalty to the Democrats was concrete. The act did little to address the systemic problems that faced blacks in areas like Chicago, Cleveland, and LA. Johnson is also reported by numerous sources as saying, "We've got to give them a little something, just enough to quiet them down, not enough to make a difference."

This was just a preview for the years to come, as Democrats on both the state and national levels have done little to attack institutional racism, despite relying on the black vote for their political success. Jimmy Carter, a democrat, won over 80% of the black vote and stayed away from policies that would benefit black people so that he wouldn't drive away his white voters. Bill Clinton was the guy who everybody called an honorary black after playing the saxophone on *The Arsenio Hall Show*. Toni Morrison opined in 1998, "Clinton displays almost every trope of blackness: single-parent household, born poor, working-class, saxophone-playing, McDonald's-and-junk-food-loving boy from Arkansas."[2] That saxophone playing junk food lover exacerbated the prison industrial complex and his administration authorized millions of people- mainly black men- to be locked away for life. Clinton also "supported the 100-to-1 sentencing disparity for crack versus powder cocaine, which produced staggering racial injustice in sentencing and boosted funding for drug-law enforcement."[3]

Even Obama, who didn't endorse policies to exclusively aid black people, said "I'm not the president of black America. I'm the president of the USA." Obama did some great things that black people were able to bond with. He developed My Brother's Keeper, he played basketball, and he created summer playlists with songs that black people actually listened to. He pardoned more non-violent criminals than any president before him, and reduced the cocaine-crack sentencing disparity from 100-1 to 18-1. But did he actively fight for ways to close the racial wealth gap, which is a component of crime in the hood? No, but he told graduates at Morehouse University not to use racism as an excuse and to be good fathers, mirroring what politicians have been condescendingly telling systematically disadvantaged black folks for years. Did he fight to dismantle systems of disadvantage that encourage crime in cities like Chicago? No. Instead, he said during the memorial of a slain Chicago teen in 2013, "There's no more important ingredient for success, nothing that would be more important for us reducing violence than strong, stable families — which means we should do more to promote marriage and encourage fatherhood." But let's love him unconditionally because he is the first black president and once sang Al Green, right?

Since the late 1800s white people have overtly and covertly tried to keep black people from voting. They employed violence to keep black people away from the polls, before giving way to literacy tests and poll taxes. When these practices were outlawed and black people largely became franchised voters, politicians became parasites. They have since recognized the value of the black voter for their own gains, often dangling a carrot in front of our faces while forcefully whipping us from behind. Honestly, it's time for those still lingering with Democrats to demand more or leave. Our votes are valuable, and politicians know this. But this isn't to say we should be headed over to the left, either. Many conservative politicians and states are actively trying to disenfranchise black voters. Since 2013, 82 restrictive voting bills have been passed in the 13 states with the highest volumes of black voters. Black people are more likely to use voter registration drives than white people; as a result, drives have become more restricted. In my home state of North Carolina, the Republican administration of former governor Pat McCrory silenced thousands of black and Latino voters. How? They conducted research on which ID's each racial demographic used to vote and then made the ID's predominately used by minorities invalid. The sole valid form of identification was the one minorities had the least of. As the president of the North Carolina chapter of the NAACP Reverend William Barber II said, "You didn't hear about fraud in North Carolina until blacks started voting in large numbers...Then all of a sudden, there's a problem with how people are voting."[4]

While it is easy to hear news like this and hate the Republican party, its not enough. Republicans definitely don't care about dismantling systems of oppression, but neither do the majority of Democrats. Instead of working to require companies to fork over better wages, regulating businesses that seek to milk us for our labor, and attacking the fused problems of segregation, gerrymandering, and housing discrimination, Democrats would prefer to throw us food stamps and cheap housing to keep our high enough above water to vote in the next election. It's time for black Americans to stop looking left or right for help and forge a new direction upward.

WILLFUL APATHY & IGNORANCE

The average black attention span is a curious thing. I know people who can whittle off sports statistics at the drop of a hat, people who know every obscure fact about their favorite celebrities, and people who have memorized every lyric from pretty much every rap song ever. I know people who think anything their favorite celebrity says is unfiltered brilliance that only few can understand. I can't count how many times I've been told Kanye is too deep for my understanding because I've called out his sporadic rants for being overrated. When I ask what exactly is so deep about a man comparing himself to Walt Disney and Michael Jackson, I'm met with silence. Me and most people have a different definition of deep. Unfortunately, some of these same people have no patience for black issues. They're the ones who hop on Twitter and chide people for "fake caring" about police brutality, discrimination, and cultural appropriation. The people who derail important discourse and hurt our community's progression. It's obvious that we can't get everyone to care, but maybe we can flip a few pillows to the cool side.

Some serious roadblocks, however, are the highly visible tastemakers and celebrities who promote ignorance and apathy. Adorned in jewels, designer clothing, and draped in the privilege that wealth and fame bring, these buffoons make indifference and ignorance to racial issues look cool. For instance, Lil Wayne, who is from the seriously racially disadvantaged city of New Orleans, said he's never experienced racism and that it doesn't exist. He later backtracked this statement, but his sentiment was clear and validated the beliefs of some of his more ignorant fans. Kanye West, who hails from the heavily redlined city of Chicago, where blacks have been targeted for over half a century, said racism is over. Perhaps he missed reports from the Department of Justice about racist law enforcement in his hometown. When asked about Mike Brown and Ferguson, Young Thug said "Leave that up with the critics and laws and all that other shit. We having fun, we iced out, we having money. That's how we doing it." This quote reflects a common theme in the black community of ignoring issues, whether willfully or on accident.

I am not saying black celebrities should be the spokespeople for black issues. I am saying that they could really spark some change by making intellectuality cool. There are black people who are suffering in this country- and many of those same people know little, or simply don't care, about the circumstances that put them there. This is dangerous because for black progression to be a true reality for most and not just some, we need people to understand and anticipate the cracks set up for them to fall through. To solve problems collectively, we must first identify them together. Bottom line? We are more valuable and strong as an informed unit. We have reached the point where we must slam our collective foot down and say no more to ignorance and apathy being marketed as cool. As we try to educate each other to the ills of systematic oppression, those who stubbornly refuse to receive knowledge should be isolated and rejected. We can't do this without irrefutably broadcasting information first. We need to make intelligence cooler than apathy, and more accessible than sports stats. We need to give people a chance to get hip to the new standard: get schooled or get left behind. After that? Every black person who willfully dodges information should be marked as an enemy to our agenda.

XRAYS, DOCTORS, & OTHER MEDICAL STUFF BLACK PEOPLE AVOID

Growing up I noticed that whenever my papa felt any type of pain, he popped an Aleve. Gout, chest pain, torn muscles, back pain, heart problems, it didn't matter. To him it was all curable with one of those tiny blue pills. My 70-year old-grandfather, like many black seniors in his age group, doesn't trust or like doctors. This isn't limited to the old folks though. Black Americans have been turning to self healing instead of doctors in time of pain for a long time now. For one thing, medical visits are cruelly expensive and not everybody has insurance. In fact, black people are less likely to have health insurance than their peers. 20% of black people are uninsured.[1] But there is also a much more sinister explanation for the general black aversion to doctors: racism and medical exploitation.

Slaves were regularly used for medical experiments with no regard for their consent. Thomas Jefferson exposed his slaves to smallpox in an effort to find a cure. J Marion Sims, touted as "the father of modern gynecology," experimented on the vaginal fistulas of at least 12 slave women without anesthesia despite its availability. In the 1930s the infamous Tuskegee Syphilis Experiment kicked off and lasted forty years. During this same time, black people who found themselves in mortal danger were kicked out of white hospitals or had to endure extremely long waits to see a white doctor for a few minutes. When patients finally got into the examination room, it wasn't always guaranteed that the doctor was sympathetic to their condition or to black people in general. The rules of white supremacy and constraints of poor education meant most patients didn't ask questions about the care they were receiving. As a result, doctors routinely did things without the consent of many of their lower class patients, but black women were special targets for sterilization. Relying on their lack of education and racial status, many states tricked poor black teens and women into giving up the ability to have children. In North Carolina, 65% of forced sterilization procedures were performed on black women, even though they only accounted for 25% of the population. In Alabama, an overwhelmingly disproportionate amount of poor black women were sought out and forced to choose between government benefits or their reproductive abilities.[2]

Then there was Henrietta Lacks, whose cervical cancer cells were scraped from inside of her and sold around the world. Her cells multiplied instead of dying, making them invaluable to medical and scientific research. Even though she died the same year her cells were taken in 1951, they lived on and built the billion-dollar medical industry while her family toiled away in harsh southern poverty. All of these exploitative and oppressive events and tactics have led to a traumatized mistrust of white doctors. We aren't exactly off the mark, either. An overwhelming number of white doctors have unmistakable bias against their black patients. In the 1990s, a study found that black Medicare recipients were less likely than their white counterparts to receive 16 of the most common hospital procedures.[3] Numerous other studies show blacks are less likely to receive necessary tests, procedures, and prescription pain medications than white people. This is goaded by the erroneous belief that black people feel less pain than everybody else. White doctors are also more likely to spend more time talking and building relationships with their white patients.

This is where someone chimes in to say "well go to black doctors!" Unfortunately, only 4% of physicians are black.[4] This low percentage is also due to systematic oppression. The medical schools of the early 1900s that were backed by the black elite were largely defunct by 1910. Upon a recommendation by "expert" Abraham Flexner to the American Medical Association (AMA) that all black medical schools except two should be closed, most black medical schools stopped attracting funding. The medical community doubted the abilities of black doctors, meaning the average black physician wannabe had slim chances of being admitted to local medical societies. To even join the AMA for certification, one had to be in a local society. Thanks to these vicious parameters, there were very few black doctors and black people who aspired to be doctors. This meant most ailing black people throughout the 20th century had to choose between apathetic white doctors or self-medicating. When you combine this little discussed facet of oppression with the cost of medical care, I unfortunately understand why my papa is so attached to his Aleve.

However, our past with doctors and the medical world isn't the only reason black people avoid preventative testing. Our reluctance is partly tied up in a stereotype about black masculinity that can have a devastating effect on health. One-third of the black male participants in a 2009 study knew someone who avoided the doctor because they believe men shouldn't go unless absolutely necessary.[5] Black men have had to be tough for centuries, and not being slowed down by physical pain has been intertwined with their identity. Visiting the doctor has never been normative for them, thanks to finance issues or discriminatory hospitals. This is unfortunate because heart disease, which is preventable 33% of the time, is the number one killer of black men. The same aforementioned study found that black men are more likely to perceive HIV as a gay virus, and are less likely to voluntarily get checked for it to avoid feeling like their masculinity has been damaged. Why is this a problem? Black men are 7x more likely than white men to get HIV. Furthermore, 87% of HIV infections among black women are attributed to heterosexual sex.

Youth Issues

Ah, the youth. Though they can be snot nosed parasitic brats, they also are stunning beacons of hope for the future. Because they actually are the future. They carry our ideas, values, and cultures with them into their creation of the next generation. But what if some of those things don't need to be embedded into the youth? What if some of the behaviors and mentalities we're introducing to our children are oppressive and toxic? The youth are where stereotypes, identity theft, unchecked mental health, and respectability politics converge.

Some of our youth issues stem from our inability to think about them as sexually autonomous beings. For instance, a lot of black parents avoid talks about sex or birth control with their teen girls to not seem like enablers. I know I'm not the only one who received frequent warnings to not be fast or to never bring a baby home. And yet, black girls are twice as likely as their white peers to be teen mothers.[1] The rate of black teen pregnancy has gone down in recent years, but still this highly preventable phenomenon remains an issue. You might be sickened to hear that STD rates on the rise among black teens. But what do you expect? Instead of hunkering down and being proactive about these sex trends, responses center around what teens should be doing instead of what they are actually doing. Bucking back against the notion of black hypersexuality, some black parents do their children a disservice by withholding information about safe sex.

Authoritarianism and secrecy go hand in hand in black families, something that many of us can attest to from personal experiences and explosive novellas ignited by brown liquor at family functions that reveal old drama that we were once too young to understand. This puts black youth at risk. The sexual abuse of black youth is a dirty and rarely discussed topic among the mainstream black community, despite the solid research exposing it's deplorable depths. Numerous studies have shown black girls are at higher risk of sexual assault and abuse than their white peers. Categorized as fast girls or good girls from childhood, a lot of sexual abuse is normalized or unreported. I was on Facebook recently and saw a former high school classmate was arrested for sleeping with a 13-year-old girl. He was at least 23, and had been abusing her for months. Instead of placing blame in the hands of a grown man who knew why his actions were wrong, my Facebook friends blamed the girl. Many were actually angry that criminal charges were even leveled in the first place. Too often adult on child sexual abuse has been normalized for both boys and girls in our community. Stereotypes rear their ugly head yet again for black boys, who are considered queer or strange for not enjoying the sexual advances or abuse of a grown woman. If a male black youth is assaulted by a man, community stigma and homophobia makes him more likely to be silent about his abuse. Both black boys and girls are at higher risk of sex trafficking than their white peers.

Sexual abuse isn't the only reality facing black youth. Teen girls are also at high risk of domestic and dating violence. The CDC reported black high school girls are 80% more likely than white girls to be hurt on purpose by a boyfriend.[2] In a community that often identifies a woman's value based on her ability to ride or die and keep a man, black girls being domestic violence targets isn't a surprising pill to swallow. In addition to teaching our girls that mean boys like them, we excuse and forgive repeat offenders like Chris Brown, Terrence Howard, and others.

I was 15 when I stumbled upon a newspaper article about a girl I went to alternative school with. She could be anybody you know. She was a normal teen when I knew her, with a big laugh and a nice personality. She lived in my neighborhood and we caught the bus together. All the boys had a crush on her and she had the type of confidence I wish I had at that age. When she was 15, her moms' ex-boyfriend stormed into their house with a gun. He murdered her mother, her brother, and managed to shoot her as she fled through a window with her 5-month-old baby sister in tow. At 15 her life was changed forever. I was going through my own drama at that age, but nothing was comparable to the injustice that girl lived through. The sickest part about this grisly story is its commonality. Black women are roughly 13% of the female population, but 50% of the annual domestic homicides.[3] This of course affects black youth tremendously. Because the police and the justice system are widely distrusted in the black community, women are more hesitant to report abuse or seek legal involvement when they need help for themselves or their children. Even if women do get a restraining order, the pieces of paper often prove useless. If women decide to leave, they're in danger. When they fight back, they often get in trouble. This goes for black youth too. Bresha Meadows was 14 when she killed her father after a lifetime of abuse. Before resorting to murdering him in his sleep, Bresha had ran away and an aunt even reported the abuse. Her mother informed the police five years before the event: "In the 17 years of our marriage, he has cut me, broke my ribs, fingers, the blood vessels in my hand, my mouth, blackened my eyes. I believe my nose was broken," she wrote. "If he finds us, I am 100 percent sure he will kill me and the children … My life is like living in a box he created for me, and if I stepped out of that box, he's there to put me back in that box."[4] After receiving no help from the government or the local community, Bresha did what she had to do. After her arrest last year, she spent six months in a detention center, and still faces jail time until her 21st birthday if convicted of aggravated murder in juvenile court.

This is rarely a topic of conversation for people who talk at length about the feminization of black men or the immorality of black women destroying the black family. How can any of us claim to be pro-black without complete concern for the welfare of black children? As black adults, we are supposed to be 100% invested in their welfare. Bad people don't become good people just because they have kids. Parenthood does not grant nobility, as much as some people would want you to believe. It should not be a surprise that misogynistic or homophobic environments turn innocent babies into hateful monsters. It should not be a surprise that these hateful monsters have their own kids and attempt to raise them in a similar way. Violence against women and queers stems from ignorance, and begins with how the kiddos are educated. It is important for black parents to chin check toxic attitudes they may be subconsciously instilling in their children. Furthermore, we are more evolved than previous generations- meaning we don't need to employ their habits of secrecy, neglect, or abuse. Things they did- inviting the funny uncle to the cookout or ignoring the bougie cousin when he slaps his wife upstairs because "that's their business"-must be talked about, targeted, and eradicated. We can thank our elders for raising us well while also pointing out how they contributed to oppressive conditions of the black experience. We can't keep doing this. We can't keep jeopardizing the safety of our children because they are the future. **71**

ZERO TOLERANCE POLICIES

When I graduated from high school approximately 11% of my senior classmates were going to college. A little more than half were graduating. I went to an extremely impoverished and predominately black school that lacked enough AP courses, resources, and caring teachers. There were some dope counselors, but they focused on who had potential. Many of the teachers were Teach for America transients, serving their two years so they could dive back into graduate school with a few paid off loans in tow. While some did care, most did not. Others simply weren't able to cope with or relate to their students.

The apathy around campus was stifling. Apathy for school and apathy for life. A large amount of my fellow seniors had either been suspended too often or had failed too many classes to qualify for college or graduation, and many didn't care. There were more security guards than there were interesting books to read in the library. Someone got shot in the parking lot moments after I was crowned homecoming queen during my senior year. Fights between campus bloods and crips were common. There were countless drug addicts and dope boys. At our very root, my peers and I weren't all that different. Most of us lived in single parent homes and received free or

& OTHER ROADBLOCKS FOR BLACK CHILDREN IN SCHOOLS

reduced lunch. Our parents didn't come up to the school unless situations were absolutely dire, and the Parent Teacher Association was less popular than the football team. The student parking lot had more empty slots than it did cars. We had all grown up in similar neighborhoods filled with cheap apartments, hood Chinese spots, and gas stations with bulletproof glass windows. We didn't come back from spring break with tans and tourist tales from exotic locales. We came back with a new piercing or tattoo, maybe, but not vacation stories. We were all the same kind of kids. And yet, I received a full scholarship to attend The Ohio State University while most of my peers went into drug enterprises, retail, or jail. Despite all of our similarities growing up, much about us was still so different. Privileged little old me had attended relatively luxurious magnet schools up to the 11th grade thanks to sheer luck from the CMS lottery system. For years a bus picked me up from various poor neighborhoods that my mother and I lived in, and shipped me all the way across town to schools with new buildings, resources, and money.

Though I often took it for granted, I went to schools with abundant extracurricular activities and caring teachers. Had I not benefitted from the lottery system, I'd have been like most of the kids at Garinger High School, who had spent their lives attending schools that never pretended to give a damn about their interests, home realities, or learning abilities. I didn't realize it until college, but many of my high school peers had been pushed through the school to prison pipeline.

It starts young. Black preschoolers are twice as likely to be suspended as their white peers for similar rule infractions.[1] According to the American Psychiatric Association, research shows black boys as young as ten are viewed as less innocent than their white peers.[2] These zero tolerance insubordination policies are even tougher in grade school, where black children continue to be suspended and expelled at disproportionate rates up to three times higher than their peers.[3] Simply showing up to school becomes discouraging when you know you'll probably get suspended for minor infractions anyways. Despite the fact that research shows building relationships with students improves behavior, school districts believe in the "out of sight" and "out of mind" approach.[4] Tardies (prevalent among low income students who work or rely on public transportation) can turn into suspensions. At my school, three class tardies were turned into a single absence and three absences earned suspensions.

At some charter schools, students are fined for infractions and suspensions. Many districts don't even require homework help or tutoring for suspended students, which causes them to fall behind. The work, by the way, often isn't relatable. The Education Improvement Act of 1984 was implemented to increase American students' exposure to black history but as many of **73** us know, the black history taught in school does little to explain present racial or economic realities that are pertinent to black students. The black experience is saved for shallow exploration in February, while stories and events from white points of view are painstakingly discussed and reviewed in English and history courses alike. Even worse, studies have shown that white teachers are implicitly biased against black students and their intelligence. In a study that observed 16,000 students, it was found that "teachers' expectations for their white students didn't differ based on the teachers' race, but that black teachers' expectations were significantly higher for their black students than white teachers' expectations were."[5]

With all of these factors at play, school becomes tedious and disenchanting, not illuminating and rewarding. It's no wonder that since 2007 the high school drop out rate of black males has been steadily increasing. In 2016, 42% of high school dropouts were black men.[6] Lacking diplomas for gainful employment, many segue into criminal activity. Don't believe me? Roughly 68% of men in prison don't have a high school diploma.[7]

I remember the semester I spent in alternative school during the 7th grade after being suspended for fighting from my highly praised performing arts academy. At Derita, teachers joked about the intelligence of students before passing out one page worksheets that were supposed to occupy us for 90 minutes. There were metal detectors at every entrance and nobody was allowed to bring anything to school with them except a folder and pencil. To this day I still don't know how one classmate regularly snuck in a cellphone. Every morning I had to flip up my bra and let my 13-year-old titties dangle under my shirt so that lecherous security guards could make sure I wasn't smuggling in contraband. I kept jolly ranchers in my underwear, but they didn't know that. At Derita there were no extracurricular activities or history lessons taught from a black point of view. Teachers did not encourage students to be better versions of themselves or ask for their opinions; they just told students to "shut up and fill out that worksheet!" They often instigated fights between students, and regularly indulged in drama with students they favored.

My semester at alternative school was just a sliver of what many black children experience for their entire academic careers. They are not groomed to be self confident critical thinkers, instead they are criminalized and rejected to make way for kids who apparently matter more than they do. The intellectual abilities of black students, particularly black boys, are underestimated or ignored in favor of their athletic or criminal potential. I remember sitting by in classes while a black male classmate would get kicked out for being a few minutes late or for passing a note. I remember security being called because a male student walked out of class to use the bathroom after being repeatedly being denied the privilege by our math teacher. I remember my civics teacher telling a JV football player that "you don't need this stuff, you've got the NFL."

America's schools are failing in general, but particularly for black children. As schools become more segregated and face even more budget cuts under the Trump administration, my concern for black children and their education has consumed me. It should consume all of us.

SO... WHAT NOW?

About that race card. It's usefulness is an illusion. White people think we enjoy pulling the race card out but what good is a single card against a loaded hand? I'm tired of the race card, damnit. I just want an equal deck and a level table to play on. In the present day, things are indeed better off than they ever have been before. But that's really not saying much. I still do not have the same opportunities, priviliges, and securities that white Americans have. Neither do the black men and women I know and love. I'd like my progeny and their offspring to have it even better than I have it. Like the mid-twentieth century era Civil Rights fighters who had it better than the 19th century abolitionists and runaway slaves before them, our generation has a duty to create better circumstances for our children. Consider the things you learned in this book going forward in your interactions with black people. Empathize with others while also attempting to educate. We can create a more level playing field for the next generation the same way our ancestors did for us. We have the advantage of vast historical and sociological knowledge that allows us to avoid traps and repetitive mistakes… if we pay attention.

Even though I connected the dots in this book for you, realize that this book is not the start or end of your journey of learning about black oppression. Oppression only becomes more complicated when one begins examining it at various intersections. For example, a disabled trans black woman will have a completely different experience to share than a cis heterosexual black man at a PWI. The number of events and people I trimmed from these pages could fill a library of books. Go and learn even more about this topic's many depths. Hopefully these essays gave you a clear idea on the basics of black oppression though, because now you've got a job to do. If you're a gossip, treat everything in this book like tabloid news that needs to be passed along to your besties. If you're not a gossip, still tell everybody. Read the books and journal articles I suggest and share those too. All the materials I listed have shaped my mind into what it is today. Many of those books are available cheaply online or are waiting to be checked out at your local library. Take the lesson even further. Print copies of certain essays in this book and let black kids dissect them with pens and highlighters. Let them grumble, let them talk it out. You can even mail this book to your racist or clueless uncle or wait until November when you can slam it down on the Thanksgiving table in front of him. My point? SHARE the knowledge inside!

You recall two heavily emphasized subjects-The Great Awakening and The Age of Enlightenment from high school history courses, right? The Great Awakening is the name used for various protestant religious revivals that have happened in America from the 18th to 20th centuries. The Age of Enlightenment (also known as the Age of Reason) often referenced to in textbooks is the period of intellectual thought and stimulation from the 18th to 19th century that promoted scientific and factual rationality over religion. The black community likes to talk about being woke, but the term itself relies on trendiness and cool points. Black America needs a Great Enlightenment. We need the entire community to be enlightened on all the issues, starting with the next generation. Enlightened from birth, throughout childhood, and for the rest of their lives. **Woke means that we're waking up from being sleep on issues. The forthcoming generations should never have to wake up- nor should they ever fall back asleep.** So we school each other and the kids. We don't rely on American schools to do give anyone the full story, let alone our children. We make them aware of America's racial history and how it has impacted the present without filters. We give them the headstart that many of us didn't have so that they can navigate America without our intraracial prejudices and propagandized misinformation weighing them down. We give them the tools of financial literacy and critical thinking, while working on our own demons. We become enlightened in all facets and develop better solutions from more evolved planes of thought. We can't afford to keep avoiding conversations about how we have been victimized because of our desire to not look like victims. Otherwise, we'll keep making mistakes getting manipulated by the system like pawns.

GLOSSARY

BLOCKBUSTING -THE SHADY ACT OF PERSUADING HOME-OWNERS TO SELL PROPERTY CHEAPLY BY EXPLOITING THEIR FEAR OF A DIFFERENT RACE OR CLASS MOVING IN AND THEN RESELLING FOR A HIGHER PRICE

CODED LANGUAGE -PASSIVE AGGRESSIVE RACIST STATE-MENTS LIKE "I'M NOT A RACIST BUT BLACK LIVES MATTER SHOULD UNDERSTAND THUGS DESERVE TO BE SHOT."

COLORISM- PREJUDICE BASED ON SHADES OF SKIN COLOR, COINED BY ALICE WALKER.

CONTRACT SELLING- PEOPLE WHO AREN'T QUALIFIED FOR LOANS INSTEAD MAKE MONTHLY PAYMENTS ON A HOME DIRECTLY TO THE SELLER WITH THE DEED ONLY GAINED WHEN THE PROPERTY IS PAID OFF ENTIRELY. NO EQUITY IS GAINED AND EVICTION IS ALWAYS LOOMING FROM LATE PAYMENTS.

DEHUMANIZATION- THE PROCESS OF STRIPPING PEOPLE OF POSITIVE HUMAN QUALITIES.

FOOD DESERT- AREAS OF THE COUNTRY DEVOID OF FRESH FRUIT, VEGGIES, AND HEALTHY FOOD. FILLED WITH FAST FOOD PLACES BUT LACKS GROCERY STORES AND FARM-ERS MARKETS

GHETTOIZATION – THE SYSTEMATIC CREATION OF DISAD-VANTAGED NEIGHBORHOODS FOR MINORITIES

IMPLICIT BIAS- ATTITUDES OR STEREOTYPES THAT AFFECT OUR UNDERSTANDING, ACTIONS, AND DECISIONS IN A SUBCONSCIOUS CAPACITY

INTERSECTIONALITY- HOW RACE, CLASS, ABILITY, AND GENDE INTERSECT AND IMPACT AN INDIVIDUAL OR GROUP,

MISOGYNOIR- MISOGYNY RESERVED FOR BLACK WOMEN BECAUSE OF THEIR RACE AND GENDER,

MICROAGRESSION- A DISMISSAL OR INSULT DIRECTED TOWARDS A MARGINALIZED GROUP BY A DOMINANT GROUP, COINED BY CHESTER M. PIERCE

NADIR OF AMERICAN RACE RELATIONS- ERA OF EXTREME RACIAL VIOLENCE FROM THE END OF RECONSTRUCTION IN 1877 TO THE EARLY 20TH CENTURY.

PATRIARCHY- GOVERNMENT OR SOCIETY IN WHICH THE FATHER IS THE HEAD OF THE FAMILY AND LAST NAMES (LINEAGE) IS PASSED DOWN THROUGH THE MALE SIDE

RACIAL PASSING- MULTI-RACIAL PERSON BECOMING WHITE FOR SURVIVAL AND/OR SOCIAL, POLITICAL, OR ECONOMIC BENEFITS. EXTREMELY PROMINENT AMONG BLACKS DURING SLAVERY AND AFTER SLAVERY WELL INTO THE MID-TWENTIETH CENTURY.

REDLINING- REFUSING LOANS, INSURANCE, AND MORT-GAGES TO PEOPLE IN AN AREA PRE-DETERMINED TO NOT BE A GOOD RISK; USUALLY BASED ON RACE

SOCIAL DEATH- THE EXPERIENCES OF PEOPLE NOT CON-SIDERED TO BE HUMAN BY MOST OF SOCIETY

STERILIZATION ABUSE- FORCING OR COERCING SOMEONE INTO GIVING UP THEIR REPRODUCTIVE RIGHTS, OR DOING IT WITHOUT THEIR KNOWLEDGE/CONSENT

WEALTH INEQUALITY- THE UNEQUAL DISTRIBUTION OF ASSETS WITHIN A POPULATION; DISPARITIES, WEALTH GAP

WHITEWASHED- EVENTS, THINGS, OR CREATIONS THAT APPEAL TO WHITE SENSIBILITIES AND/OR GUILT, AT THE COST OF ERASING OTHER KINDS OF PEOPLE

SUGGESTED READING

BOOKS

BLACK MAN IN A WHITE COAT (DAMON TWEEDY, MD)

A CHOSEN EXILE: HISTORY OF RACIAL PASSING IN AMERICAN LIFE (ALLYSON HOBBS)

KILLING THE BLACK BODY (DOROTHY ROBERTS)

BLACK STATS (MONIQUE W MORRIS)

POST TRAUMATIC SLAVE SYNDROME (JOY DEGRUY, PH.D.)

WOMEN, RACE, AND CLASS (ANGELA DAVIS)

THE IMMORTAL LIFE OF HENRIETTA LACKS (REBECCA SKLOOT)

DISINTEGRATION: THE SPLINTERING OF BLACK AMERICA (EUGENE ROBINSON)

A PEOPLES HISTORY OF THE UNITED STATES (HOWARD ZINN)

FAMILY PROPERTIES: HOW THE STRUGGLE OVER RACE AND REAL ESTATE TRANSFORMED CHICAGO AND URBAN AMERICA (BERYL SATTER)

WHY ARE ALL THE BLACK KIDS SITTING TOGETHER IN THE CAFETERIA: AND OTHER CONVERSATIONS ABOUT RACE (BEVERLY DANIEL TATUM)

BLACK LIKE ME (JOHN HOWARD GRIFFITH)

GETTING PLAYED: AFRICAN AMERICAN GIRLS, URBAN INEQUALITY, AND GENDERED VIOLENCE (JODY MILLER)

MEDICAL APARTHEID: THE DARK HISTORY OF MEDICAL EXPERIMENTATION FROM COLONIAL TIMES TO THE PRESENT (HARRIET A WASHINGTON)

THE NEW JIM CROW: MASS INCARCERATION IN THE AGE OF COLORBLINDNESS (MICHELLE ALEXANDER)

BLACK AGAINST EMPIRE: THE HISTORY AND THE POLITICS OF THE BLACK PANTHER PARTY (JOSHUA BLOOM AND WALDO E. MARTIN)

NEGROLAND (MARGOT JEFFERSON)

FORTY MILLION DOLLAR SLAVES: THE RISE, FALL, AND REDEMPTION OF THE BLACK ATHLETE (WILLIAM C RHODEN)

LIVING FOR THE CITY: MIGRATION, EDUCATION, AND THE RISE OF THE BLACK PANTHER PARTY IN OAKLAND, CALIFORNIA (DONNA JEAN MURCH)

SALTWATER SLAVERY (STEPHANIE SMALLWOOD)

THE FIRE NEXT TIME (JAMES BALDWIN)

WHY AMERICANS HATE WELFARE: RACE, MEDIA, AND THE POLITICS OF ANTI-POVERTY POLICY (MARTIN GILENS)

WHEN AND WHERE I ENTER: THE IMPACT OF BLACK WOMANHOOD ON RACE AND SEX IN AMERICA (PAULA GIDDINGS)

COOL POSE: THE DILEMMA OF BLACK MANHOOD IN AMERICA (RICHARD MAJORS AND JANET MANCINI BILLSON)

ASSATA (ASSATA SHAKUR)

VOICES FROM SLAVERY: 100 AUTHENTIC SLAVE NARRATIVES (EFITED BY NORMAN R. YETMAN)

THE MISEDUCATION OF THE NEGRO (CARTER G WOODSON)

COMING OF AGE IN MISSISSIPPI (ANNE MOODY)

BLACK AMERICAN MONEY (DR. BOYCE WATKINS)

JOURNALS, ARTICLES, AND WEB DATABASES

CINETHETIC RACISM: WHITE REDEMPTION AND BLACK STEREOTYPES IN "MAGICAL NEGRO" FILMS (MATTHEW W. HUGHEY)

BLACK MUSICIANS FROM SLAVERY TO FREEDOM (PAUL A CIMBALA)

ARISTOCRATS OF COLOR (WALTER B HILL JR)

LOOKING AT THE STARS: THE BLACK PRESS, AFRICAN AMERICAN CELEBRITY CULTURE, AND CRITICAL CITIZENSHIP IN EARLY 20TH CENTURY AMERICA (CARRIE TERESA)

RACE AND PUNISHMENT: RACIAL PERCEPTIONS OF CRIME AND SUPPORT FOR PUNITIVE POLICIES (THE SENTENCING PROJECT)

THE CASE FOR REPARATIONS (TA-NEHISI COATES)

WHITE PRIVILEGE: UNPACKING THE INVISIBLE KNAPSACK (PEGGY MCINTOSH)

AGE, RACE, CLASS, AND SEX: WOMEN REDEFINING DIFFERENCE (AUDRE LORD)

BLACK LIVES MATTER: THE SCHOTT 50 STATE REPORT ON PUBLIC EDUCATION AND BLACK MALES

BENDING THE BARS OF EMPIRE FROM EVERY GHETTO FOR SURVIVAL: THE BLACK PANTHER PARTY'S RADICAL ANTIHUNGER POLITICS OF SOCIAL REPRODUCTION AND SCALE (NIK HEYNEN)

REFERENCE LIST

Buyers Not Owners
1. Alcorn, C. L. (2016, September 01). Black Businesses Are on the Rise in the U.S. Retrieved April 20, 2017, from http://fortune.com/2016/09/01/black-businesses-us/
2. Morris, M. W. (2014). Black stats: African Americans by the numbers. New York: The New Press.

Christianity and Black Forgiveness
1. Bowditch, W. I. (1849). Slavery and the Constitution (p. 53). Boston, MA: R. F. Wallcut.
2. Drayton, W. (1836). The South Vindicated from the Treason and Fanaticism of the Northern Abolitionists (p. 71). Philadelphia, PA: H. Manly.
3. Liu, J. (2009, January 29). A Religious Portrait of African-Americans. Retrieved April 20, 2017, from http://www.pewforum.org/2009/01/30/a-religious-portrait-of-african-americans/

Divisions
1. N. (2007). On Slaveholders Sexual Abuse of Slaves: Selections from 19th-&20th-Century Slave Narratives. Retrieved from http://nationalhumanitiescenter.org/pds/maai/enslavement/text6/masterslavesexualabuse.pdf
2. Ibid. ^^^
3. Bardaglio, P. W. (1994). Rape and the Law in the Old South: "Calculated to excite Indigna tion in every heart". The Journal of Southern History, 60(4), 754. doi:10.2307/2211066
4. Phillips, K. L. (2012). Daily life during African American migrations. Santa Barbara, CA: Greenwood.

Entertainers and Athletes
1. Juli Jones, Jr., "In the squared circle: Battling Siki," Chicago Defender, March 17, 1923, 10
2. Teresa, C. Looking at the Stars: The Black Press, African American Celebrity Culture, and Critical Citizenship in Early Twentieth Century America, 1895-1935 (Doctoral disserta tion) [Abstract].
3. Morris, M. W. (2014). Black stats: African Americans by the numbers. New York: The New Press.
4. Duberman, Martin B. (1989). Paul Robeson. Bodley Head. ISBN 978-0-370-30575-2.
5. Morris, M. W. (2014). Black stats: African Americans by the numbers. New York: The New Press.

Financial Disadvantages
1. Shin, L. (2016, January 25). The Racial Wealth Gap: Why A Typical White Household Has 16 Times The Wealth Of A Black One. Retrieved April 21, 2017, from https://www.forbes.com/sites/laurashin/2015/03/26/the-racial-wealth-gap-why-a-typical-white-household-has-16-times-the-wealth-of-a-black-one/#5a3f1e881f45
2. Morris, M. W. (2014). Black stats: African Americans by the numbers. New York: The New Press.
3. Ibid.^^^
4. Ibid.^^^

Housing Discrimination
1. Satter, B. (2009). The Noose Around Black Chicago. In Family Properties:How the Struggle Over Race and Real Estate Transformed Chicago and Urban America. New York, NY: Henry Holt and Company, LLC .
2. Ibid.^^^
3. Powell, M. (2009, June 6). Bank Accused of Pushing Mortgage Deals on Blacks. New York Times. Retrieved February 20, 2017.

Justice System Blues
1. Yetman, N. R. (2000). Voices from slavery: 100 authentic slave narratives. Mineola, NY: Dover Publications.
2. Negro Vagrant. (1882, June 30). Semi-Weekly Interior Journal. Retrieved February 20, 2017
3. Morris, M. W. (2014). Black stats: African Americans by the numbers. New York: The New Press.
4. Kutateladze, B. L., & Andiloro, N. R. (2014). Prosecution & Racial Justice in New York County (Tech. No. 247227).

5. Abrams, D. S., Bertrand, M., & Mullainathan, S. (2012). Do Judges Vary in Their Treatment of Race? The Journal of Legal Studies, 41(2), 347-383. doi:10.1086/666006

6. Markowitz, E. (2016, January 25). Louisiana, 'Prison Capital' Of The World, Hosts Biggest US Prison Convention. Retrieved February 21, 2017, from http://www.ibtimes.com/louisiana-prison-capital-world-hosts-biggest-us-prison-convention-2278102

7. Michael Sallah, Robert O'Harrow Jr. and Steven Rich. (2014, September 08). Police seizure of motorists' cash on rise, netting $2.5 billion since 9/11. http://www.chicagotribune.com/classified/automotive/sns-wp-washpost-bc-forfeiture-1-repeat06-20140906-story.html

8. Balko, R. (2014, February 18). The Drug War's Profit Motive. The Washington Post. Retrieved April 20, 2017, from http://www.highbeam.com/doc/1P2-35714543.html?refid=easy_hf

8. Alexander, M. (2016). New jim crow: mass incarceration in the age of colorblindness. New Press.

Killing The Black Body

1. Edwards, J. (2011, January 05). Why Big Tobacco Targeted Blacks With Ads for Menthol Cigarettes. Retrieved April 20, 2017, from http://www.cbsnews.com/news/why-big-tobacco-targeted-blacks-with-ads-for-menthol-cigarettes/

2. ibid, ^^^

3. Jones, L. (2010, December 14). Jury Awards $71M In Free Cigarette Samples Lawsuit. http://boston.cbslocal.com/2010/12/14/jury-awards-71m-in-free-cigarette-samples-lawsuit/

4. McNichol, T. (2011, March 25). Mint That Kills: The Curious Life of Menthol Cigarettes. Retrieved April 20, 2017, from https://www.theatlantic.com/health/archive/2011/03/mint-that-kills-the-curious-life-of-menthol-cigrettes/73016/

5. Erickson, J. (2016, January 19). Targeting minority, low-income neighborhoods for hazardous waste sites. Retrieved February 20, 2017, from http://ns.umich.edu/new/releases/23414-targeting-minority-low-income-neighborhoods-for-hazardous-waste-sites

6. Morris, M. W. (2014). Black stats: African Americans by the numbers. New York: The New Press.

7. Luzuriaga, T. D. (2008, April 3). Alcohol more available in poor, black areas. The Boston Globe. http://archive.boston.com/news/local/articles/2008/04/03/alcohol_more_available_in_poor_black_ areas/

Murdering and Discrediting Black Leaders and Movements

1. Abu-Jamal, M. (2004). We want freedom: a life in the Black Panther Party. Brooklyn, NY: Common Notions.

Negative Representations in The News

1. Williams, E. H. (1914, February 8). Negro Cocaine "Fiends" New Southern Menace. The New York Times.

2. Gilens, M. (2003). How The Poor Became Black. In Race and the Politics of Welfare Reform. Ann Arbor, MI: The University of Michigan Press.

3. Drum, K. (2016, March 3). A very brief history of super-predators. Retrieved February 20, 2017, from http://www.motherjones.com/kevin-drum/2016/03/very-brief-history-super-predators

4. Ingraham, C. (2014, August 25). Three quarters of whites don't have any non-white friends. Retrieved April 20, 2017, from https://www.washingtonpost.com/news/wonk/wp/2014/08/25/three-quarters-of-whites-dont-have-any-non-white-friends/?utm_term=.4b0df318e280

Police Brutality

1. Kindy, K., Tate, A. R., Jenkins, J., Rich, S., Alexander, K. L., & Lowery, W. (2015, May 30). Fatal police shootings in 2015 approaching 400 nationwide. Retrieved April 20, 2017, from https://www.washingtonpost.com/national/fatal-police-shootings-in-2015-approaching-400-nationwide/2015/05/30/d322256a-058e-11e5-a428-c984eb077d4e_story.html?utm_term=.99aac3892b5e

2. Ferner, M., & Wing, N. (2016, January 13). Here's How Many Cops Got Convicted Of Murder Last Year For On-Duty Shootings. Retrieved April 20, 2017, from http://www.huffingtonpost.com/entry/police-shooting-convictions_us_5695968ce4b086bc1cd5d0da

Quadroons, Mulattos, and Other Tentacles of Colorism

1. Wayne, M. (2014). Imagining Black America. New Haven: Yale Univ. Press.

Toms and Traitors

1. Satter, B. (2009). The Noose Around Black Chicago. In Family Properties:How the Struggle Over Race and Real Estate Transformed Chicago and Urban America. New York, NY: Henry Holt and Company, LLC .

Unchecked Mental Health

1. Morris, M. W. (2014). Black stats: African Americans by the numbers. New York: The New Press.

2. Hamm, N. (2014, September 25). High Rates of Depression Among African-American Women, Low Rates of Treatment. http://www.huffingtonpost.com/nia-hamm/depression-african-american-wom

81

en_b_5836320.html

3. American Psychological Association. (n.d.). Health Disparities and Mental/Behavioral Workforce. Retrieved February 20, 2017, from http://www.apa.org/about/gr/issues/workforce/disparity.aspx

4. Behind Mental Health Stigmas In Black Communities. (2012, August 20). http://www.npr.org/2012/08/20/159376802/behind-mental-health-stigmas-in-black-communities

5. Walker, D. (2016, June 15). As Suicide Rates For Black Children Rise, Protecting Emotional Heath Is Vital. http://www.ebony.com/wellness-empowerment/black-suicide-rates#axzz4eqyGw7fi

6. Morris, M. W. (2014). Black stats: African Americans by the numbers. New York: The New Press.

Voter Use and Abuse

1. Oreskes, M. (1989, July 01). Civil Rights Act Leaves Deep Mark On the American Political Landscape. http://www.nytimes.com/1989/07/02/us/civil-rights-act-leaves-deep-mark-on-the-american-political-landscape.html?pagewanted=all

2. Morrison, T. (2016, August 01). On the First Black President. Retrieved January 21, 2017, from http://www.newyorker.com/magazine/1998/10/05/comment-6543

3. Alexander, M. (2016). New jim crow: mass incarceration in the age of colorblindness.

4. Wan, W. (2016, September 02). How Republicans in North Carolina created a 'monster' voter ID law. Retrieved February 21, 2017, from http://www.chicagotribune.com/news/nationworld/politics/ct-north-carolina-voter-id-law-20160902-story.html

X Rays and Other Medical Things Black People Avoid

1. Morris, M. W. (2014). Black stats: African Americans by the numbers. New York: The New Press.

2. Krase, K. (2014, October 1). History of Forced Sterilization and Current U.S. Abuses. Retrieved January 21, 2017, from http://www.ourbodiesourselves.org/health-info/forced-sterilization/

3. National Research Council (US) Panel on Race, Ethnicity, and Health in Later Life; Bulatao RA, Anderson NB, editors. Understanding Racial and Ethnic Differences in Health in Late Life: A Research Agenda. Washington (DC): National Academies Press (US); 2004. 10, Health Care. Available from: https://www.ncbi.nlm.nih.gov/books/NBK24693/

4. Morris, M. W. (2014). Black stats: African Americans by the numbers. New York: The New Press.

5. Duck, W. (2009). Black Male Sexual Politics: Avoidance of HIV/AIDS Testing as a Masculine Health Practice. Journal of African American Studies, 13(3), 283-306.

Youth Issues

1. Fox, M. (2016, April 28). Teen Birth Rates Plummet Among Blacks, Latinas: CDC. http://www.nbcnews.com/health/sexual-health/teen-birth-rates-plummet-among-blacks-hispanics-cdc-n564291 O'Hara, M. E. (2017, April 11).

2. Black youth most affected by teen dating violence. (2012, February 9). http:/thegrio.com/2012/02/29/black-teens-most-affected-by-teen-dating-violence/

3. Domestic Violence: Nearly Three U.S. Women Killed Every Day by Intimate Partners. http://www.nbcnews.comnews/us-news/domestic-violence-nearly-three-u-s-women- killed-every-day-n745166

4. Jeltsen, M. (2016, August 08). 14-Year-Old Girl Accused Of Killing Her Allegedly Abusive Father. http://www.huffingtonpost.com/entry/bresha-meadows-ohio-girl-kills-father_us_57a7649ee4b021fd9878e653

Zero Tolerance Policies

1. Young, Y. (2016, October 04). Teachers' implicit bias against black students starts in preschool, study finds. https://www.theguardian.com/world/2016/oct/04/black-students-teachers-implicit-racial-bias-preschool-study

2. American Psychiatric Assiciation. (2014, March 6). Black Boys Viewed as Older, Less Innocent Than Whites, Research Finds. http://www.apa.org/news/press/releases/2014/03/black-boys-older.aspx

3. Wald, J., & Losen, D. J. (2003). Defining and redirecting a school-to-prison pipeline. New Directions for Youth Development, 2003(99), 9-15. doi:10.1002/yd.51

4. Green, A. (2015, August 26). When Schools Are Forced to Practice Race-Based Discipline. https://www.theatlantic.com/education/archive/2015/08/teachers-say-no-disparate-impact-discipline/402144/

5. Nelson, L. (2015, August 19). Racism in the classroom: the "soft bigotry of low expectations" is just regular bigotry. http://www.vox.com/policy-and-politics/2015/8/19/9178573/teacher-students-race-study

6. Williams, J. (2015, February 11). Black Brains Matter: Why Are Graduation Rates So Low? Retrieved February 21, 2017, from http://www.takepart.com/article/2015/02/11/black-brains-matter-why-are-graduation-rates-so-low

7. Hanson, K., & Stipek, D. (2014, May 15). Schools v. prisons: Education's the way to cut prison population. http:/www.mercurynews.com/2014/05/15/schools-v-prisons-educations-the-way-to-cut-prison-population/

ABOUT THE AUTHOR:

ELEXUS JIONDE

You can call her Elexus or Lexual. She was born on January 26th 1994. She graduated from The Ohio State University in August 2016 and holds a B.A. in history. She plans to go back for her masters eventually.

Elexus always loved history and social commentary, but on September 11th 2016, everything got thrown into high gear. She tweeted a history thread about white supremacy and black oppression on that day that has since gone viral. When she's not doing Intelexual Media work....

She loves to travel, learn, cook, and eat good food. Yup, she's boring...

.....But not really. She plans on writing a memoir....

....and eventually buying a puppy.

This is her first book.

@Lexual__
@IntelexualMedia

CONTRIBUTORS

PHOTOGRAPHY:
ChrisP Images

COVER MODEL:
Chasity Samone

MALE MODEL:
Justin Hampton

ILLUSTRATIONS:
BAGJUICECO.
Briana Odlum and Nigel Hylton

(Letters B, C, D, G, H, I, J (chaingang) ,L, M, N, O, P, R, S, Z, & Conclusion)

BYKYRIE
(Letters E, F, J (handcuffs), K, Q, U, X, & Reading Suggestions)

Made in the USA
Middletown, DE
25 April 2017